U.S. Department
of Transportation

**Federal Aviation
Administration**

M000299838

Flight Instructor
Practical Test Standards
for
Airplane

June 2012
(Effective December 1, 2012)

Flight Standards Service
Washington, DC 20591

(this page intentionally left blank)

Flight Instructor
Airplane
Practical Test Standards

2012

Flight Standards Service
Washington, DC 20591

(this page intentionally left blank)

Note

Material in FAA-S-8081-6D will be **effective December 1, 2012**. All previous editions of Flight Instructor – Airplane Practical Test Standards will be obsolete as of this date.

(this page intentionally left blank)

Foreword

The Flight Instructor—Airplane Practical Test Standards book has been published by the Federal Aviation Administration (FAA) to establish the standards for the flight instructor certification practical tests for the airplane category and the single-engine and multiengine classes. FAA inspectors and designated pilot examiners shall conduct practical tests in compliance with these standards. Flight instructors and applicants should find these standards helpful in practical test preparation.

6/29/2012
/s/ Leslie Smith for
John Allen, Director
Flight Standards Service

(this page intentionally left blank)

Record of Changes

Change 1 (September 20, 2012)

- Removed references to LORAN from the following:

  o "Abbreviations" section of Introduction
  o Objective 1 in Task L (Navigation Systems and Radar Services) of Section 1, Area of Operation II – Technical Subject Areas
  o Objective 1 in Task L (Navigation Aids and Radar Services) of Section 2, Area of Operation II – Technical Subject Areas

Change 2 (November 21, 2012)

- Revised Note in "Aircraft and Equipment Required for the Practical Test" section of Introduction regarding use of non-complex airplanes during renewal or reinstatement of the Flight Instructor Certificate.
- Revised Note in "Renewal or Reinstatement of a Flight Instructor Certificate" section of Introduction regarding use of non-complex airplanes during renewal or reinstatement of the Flight Instructor Certificate.

Change 3 (January 28, 2013)

- Revised the "Practical Test Prerequisites" section of the Introduction regarding the amount of time for which an endorsement from an authorized flight instructor may be used to apply for an initial certification or additional rating practical test.

Change 4 (January 15, 2015)

- Revised Note in "Aircraft and Equipment Required for the Practical Test" section of Introduction and added paragraph 4 clarifying when a non-complex airplane is required for the practical test. These edits are intended to make clear that a complex aircraft is not required when adding an airplane class rating to an existing flight instructor certificate that already contains an airplane category and class rating. The FAA finds the requirements for the use of a complex airplane are not necessary when the applicant has already satisfactorily demonstrated the takeoff, landing, emergency, and other Tasks contained within this PTS in a complex airplane.

  o For example, an applicant seeking to add a single-engine rating to an existing flight instructor certificate that already contains an airplane multiengine category and class rating does not need to perform the practical test in a complex airplane.

- Restored Objective 2 in Task F (Secondary Stalls (Demonstration)(ASEL and ASES)) of Section 1, Area of Operation XI – Slow Flights, Stalls, and Spins.

  o Previously removed inadvertently.

Change 5 (June 17, 2016)

- Updated all references throughout the document that referred to the Private Pilot Airplane Practical Test Standards (FAA-S-8081-14) to refer to the superseding Private Pilot – Airplane Airman Certification Standards (FAA-S-ACS-6).

Change 6 (April 19, 2018)

- Removed the complex airplane requirement from practical tests for an airplane single-engine instructor rating and made corresponding changes to Task elements and the following sections in the Introduction:

  o "Aircraft and Equipment Required for the Practical Test"
  o "Renewal or Reinstatement of a Flight Instructor Certificate"
  o

Major Enhancements to Version FAA-S-8081-6D

Introduction

- References updated
- "Special Emphasis Areas" section updated to include reference to runway incursion avoidance
- "Flight Instructor Responsibility" section updated to include reference to runway incursion avoidance
- "Examiner Responsibility" section updated to include reference to runway incursion avoidance
- "Satisfactory Performance" section updated to include reference to runway incursion mitigation techniques
- "Aeronautical Decision Making and Risk Management" section updated
- "Use or Distractions During Practical Test" section updated
- "Renewal or Reinstatement of a Flight instructor Certificate" section updated

Section 1, Flight Instructor – Airplane Single-Engine

- Area of Operation I updated to comply with FAA-H-8083-9A, "Aviation Instructor's Handbook"
- Area of Operation II updated to include Task B: "Runway Incursion Avoidance"
- Area of Operation V, Task D: "Taxiing – Landplane" updated to include runway incursion language
- Area of Operation VI, Task A: "Radio Communications and ATC Light Signals" updated to include non-towered airports procedures
- Area of Operation VII, Task F: "Normal and Crosswind Approach and Landing" updated to include runway incursion language

Section 2, Flight Instructor – Airplane Multiengine

- Area of Operation I updated to comply with FAA-H-8083-9A, "Aviation Instructor's Handbook"
- Area of Operation II updated to include Task B: "Runway Incursion Avoidance"
- Area of Operation V, Task D: "Taxiing – Landplane" updated to include runway incursion language
- Area of Operation VI, Task A: "Radio Communications and ATC Light Signals" updated to include non-towered airports procedures

- Area of Operation VII, Task E: "Normal and Crosswind Approach and Landing" updated to include runway incursion language

Table of Contents

(this page intentionally left blank)

Introduction

General Information

The Flight Standards Service of the Federal Aviation Administration (FAA) has developed this practical test as the standard to be used by examiners[1] when conducting flight instructor airplane practical tests. Instructors are expected to address all of the elements contained in this practical test standard (PTS) when preparing applicants for practical tests. Applicants should be familiar with this PTS and refer to these standards during their training.

The FAA gratefully acknowledges the valuable assistance provided by many individuals, companies, and organizations throughout the aviation community who have contributed their time and talent in assisting with the revision of this practical test standard.

This book may be purchased from the Superintendent of Documents, U.S. Government Printing Office (GPO), Washington, DC 20402-9325, or from GPO's web site, http://bookstore.gpo.gov.

This PTS is also available for download, in pdf format, from the Flight Standards Service web site, www.faa.gov.

This PTS is published by the U.S. Department of Transportation, Federal Aviation Administration, Airman Testing Standards Branch, AFS-630, P.O. Box 25082, Oklahoma City, OK 73125.

Comments regarding this publication should be sent, in e-mail form, to AFS630comments@faa.gov.

Practical Test Standards Concept

Title 14 of the Code of Federal Regulations (14 CFR) part 61 specifies the Areas of Operation in which knowledge and skill must be demonstrated by the applicant before the issuance of a flight instructor certificate with the associated category and class ratings. The Code of Federal Regulations provides the flexibility that permits the FAA to publish practical test standards containing the Areas of Operation and specific Tasks in which competency must be demonstrated. The FAA will revise this book whenever it is determined that changes are needed in the interest of safety. **Adherence to the provisions of regulations and the practical**

---

1 The word "examiner" denotes either the FAA inspector, FAA designated pilot examiner, or other authorized person who conducts the practical test.

test standards is mandatory for the evaluation of flight instructor applicants.

Flight Instructor Practical Test Book Description

This book contains the practical test standards for Flight Instructor—Airplane (single-engine and multiengine). Other flight instructor practical test books include:

- FAA-S-8081-7, Flight Instructor—Rotorcraft – Helicopter and Gyroplane
- FAA-S-8081-8, Flight Instructor—Glider
- FAA-S-8081-9, Flight Instructor—Instrument – Airplane and Helicopter

The Flight Instructor Practical Test Standards include the Areas of Operation and Tasks for the issuance of an initial flight instructor certificate, for the addition of category and/or class ratings to that certificate, and for renewal or reinstatement of a certificate or rating by a practical test.

Flight Instructor Practical Test Standards Description

Areas of Operation are phases of the practical test. In this practical test book, the first Area of Operation is Fundamentals of Instructing; the last is Postflight Procedures. The examiner may conduct the practical test in any sequence that will result in a complete and efficient test; **however, the ground portion of the practical test must be completed prior to the flight portion.**

Tasks are titles of knowledge areas, flight procedures, or maneuvers appropriate to an Area of Operation. The abbreviation(s) within parentheses immediately following a Task refer to the category and/or class aircraft appropriate to that Task. The meaning of each abbreviation is as follows:

ASEL	Airplane—Single-Engine Land
AMEL	Airplane—Multiengine Land
ASES	Airplane—Single-Engine Sea
AMES	Airplane—Multiengine Sea

Note: *When administering a test based on sections 1 and 2 of this PTS, the Tasks appropriate to the class airplane (ASEL, ASES, AMEL, or AMES) used for the test must be included in the plan of action. The absence of a class indicates the Task is for all classes.*

Note is used to emphasize special considerations required in the Area of Operation or Task.

Reference identifies the publication(s) that describe(s) the Task. Descriptions of Tasks and maneuver tolerances are not included in these standards because this information can be found in the current issue of the listed reference. Publications other than those listed may be used for references if their content conveys substantially the same meaning as the referenced publications.

These practical test standards are based on the following references:

14 CFR part 1	Definitions and Abbreviations
14 CFR part 23	Airworthiness Standards: Normal, Utility, Acrobatic, and Commuter Category Airplanes
14 CFR part 39	Airworthiness Directives
14 CFR part 43	Maintenance, Preventive Maintenance, Rebuilding, and Alteration
14 CFR part 61	Certification: Pilots and Flight Instructors
14 CFR part 67	Medical Standards and Certification
14 CFR part 91	General Operating and Flight Rules
NTSB part 830	Notification and Reporting of Aircraft Accidents and Incidents
AC 00-6	Aviation Weather
AC 00-45	Aviation Weather Services
AC 60-22	Aeronautical Decision Making
AC 60-28	English Language Skill Standards as required by 14 CFR parts 61, 63, and 65
AC 61-65	Certification: Pilots and Flight Instructors
AC 61-67	Stall and Spin Awareness Training
AC 61-84	Role of Preflight Preparation
AC 61-94	Pilot Transition Course for Self-Launching or Powered Sailplanes (Motorgliders)
AC 61-107	Operations of Aircraft at Altitude above 25,000 Feet MSL and/or Mach Numbers (M_{MO}) Greater Than .75
AC 90-42	Traffic Advisory Practices at Airports without Operating Control Towers
AC 90-48	Pilots' Role in Collision Avoidance
AC 90-66	Recommended Standard Traffic Patterns for Aeronautical Operations at Airports without Operating Control Towers
AC 91-13	Cold Weather Operation of Aircraft

AC 91-55	Reduction of Electrical System Failures Following Aircraft Engine Starting
AC 91-73	Parts 91 and 135 Single-Pilot Procedures During Taxi Operations
FAA-H-8083-1	Aircraft Weight and Balance Handbook
FAA-H-8083-2	Risk Management Handbook
FAA-H-8083-3	Airplane Flying Handbook
FAA-H-8083-9	Aviation Instructor's Handbook
FAA-S-ACS-6	Private Pilot – Airplane Airman Certification Standards
FAA-S-8081-4	Instrument Rating Practical Test Standards
FAA-S-8081-12	Commercial Pilot Practical Test Standards
FAA-H-8083-15	Instrument Flying Handbook
FAA-H-8083-23	Seaplane, Skiplane, and Float/Ski Equipped Helicopter Operations Handbook
FAA-H-8083-25	Pilot's Handbook of Aeronautical Knowledge
Order 8080.6	Conduct of Airman Knowledge Tests
AC 150/5340-1	Standards for Airport Markings
AC 150/5340-18	Standards for Airport Sign Systems
AC 150/5340-30	Design and Installation Details for Airport Visual Aids
AIM	Aeronautical Information Manual
A/FD	Airport/Facility Directory
NOTAMs	Notices to Airmen
POH/AFM	Pilot Operating Handbooks and FAA-Approved Airplane Flight Manuals
USCG	COMDTINST M16672.2 United States Coast Guard Commandant Instruction, Navigation Rule: International-Inland

The Objective lists the elements that must be satisfactorily performed to demonstrate competency in a Task. The Objective includes:

1. Specifically what the applicant should be able to do.
2. Conditions under which the Task is to be performed.
3. Acceptable performance standards.

The examiner determines that the applicant meets the Task Objective through the demonstration of competency in all elements of knowledge and/or skill unless otherwise noted. The Objectives of Tasks in certain Areas of Operation, such as Fundamentals of Instructing and Technical Subjects, include only knowledge elements. Objectives of Tasks in Areas of Operation that include elements of skill, as well as knowledge, also include common errors, which the applicant must be able to describe, recognize, analyze, and correct.

The Objective of a Task that involves pilot skill consists of four parts. The four parts include determination that the applicant exhibits:

1.   Instructional knowledge of the elements of a Task (accomplished through descriptions, explanations, and simulated instruction).
2.   Instructional knowledge of common errors related to a Task, including their recognition, analysis, and correction.
3.   The ability to demonstrate and simultaneously explain the key elements of a Task at the Commercial Pilot skill level[2].
4.   The ability to analyze and correct common errors related to a Task.

Abbreviations

14 CFR	Title 14 of the Code of Federal Regulations
AC	Advisory Circular
ADM	Aeronautical Decision Making
AGL	Above Ground Level
AIRMETS	Airman's Meteorological Information
AM	Automation Management
AME	Airplane Multiengine
AMEL	Airplane Multiengine Land
AMES	Airplane Multiengine Sea
ASEL	Airplane Singe-Engine Land
ASES	Airplane Single-Engine Sea
ATC	Air Traffic Control
ATIS	Automatic Terminal Information Service
CFIT	Controlled Flight into Terrain
CRM	Crew Resource Management
DME	Distance Measuring Equipment
FAA	Federal Aviation Administration

---

[2] The teaching techniques and procedures should conform to those set forth in FAA-H-8083-25, Pilot's Handbook of Aeronautical Knowledge; FAA-H-8083-9, Aviation Instructor's Handbook; FAA-H-8083-3, Airplane Flying Handbook; and FAA-H-8083-15, Instrument Flying Handbook.

FDC	Flight Data Center

Change 1 (9/20/2012)

FSDO	Flight Standards District Office
G	Glider
GPO	Government Printing Office
GPS	Global Positioning System
IA	Instrument Airplane
IH	Instrument Helicopter
LAHSO	Land and Hold Short Operations
MEL	Minimum Equipment List
M$_{MO}$	Maximum Operating Limit Speed
NAVAID	Navigation Aid
NDB	Non Directional Beacon
NOTAM	Notice to Airmen
NTSB	National Transportation Safety Board
NWS	National Weather Service
PC	Proficiency Check
PTS	Practical Test Standard
RG	Rotorcraft Gyroplane
RH	Rotorcraft Helicopter
RM	Risk Management
SA	Situational Awareness
SIGMETS	Significant Meteorological Advisory
SUA	Special Use Airspace
TFR	Temporary Flight Restriction
TM	Task Management
VFR	Visual Flight Rules
VHF	Very High Frequency
VOR	Very High Frequency Omnirange
V$_{MC}$	Minimum Control Speed with the Critical Engine Inoperative
V$_{MO}$	Maximum Operating Limit Speed (Knots)
V$_{SSE}$	Safe Single-Engine Speed
V$_X$	Best Angle of Climb
V$_Y$	Best Rate of Climb
V$_{YSE}$	Single-Engine Best Rate of Climb

Use of the Practical Test Standards Book

The Flight Instructor Practical Test Standards are designed to evaluate competency in both knowledge and skill.

The FAA requires that all Flight Instructor practical tests be conducted in accordance with the appropriate Flight Instructor Practical Test Standards and the policies set forth in the Introduction. The flight instructor applicant must be prepared to demonstrate the ability to instruct effectively in **all** Tasks included in the Areas of Operation of the appropriate practical test standards, unless otherwise noted.

All of the procedures and maneuvers in the Private Pilot and Commercial Pilot Practical Test Standards have been included in the Flight Instructor Practical Test Standards. **However, the flight instructor PTS allows the examiner to select one or more Tasks in each Area of Operation, therefore allowing the practical test for initial certification to be completed within a reasonable time frame.** In certain Areas of Operation, there are **required** Tasks, which the examiner must select. These required Tasks are identified by Notes immediately following the Area of Operation titles.

The term "instructional knowledge" means the instructor applicant is capable of using the appropriate reference to provide the "application or correlative level of knowledge" of a subject matter topic, procedure, or maneuver. It also means that the flight instructor applicant's discussions, explanations, and descriptions should follow the recommended teaching procedures and techniques explained in FAA-H-8083-9, Aviation Instructor's Handbook.

In preparation for the practical test, the examiner must develop a written "plan of action" for each practical test. The plan of action is a tool, for the sole use of the examiner, to be used in evaluating the applicant. The plan of action need not be grammatically correct or in any formal format. The plan of action for an initial certification test includes one or more Tasks in each Area of Operation and **always** includes the required Tasks. The plan of action must incorporate one or more scenarios that will be used during the practical test. The examiner should try to include as many of the Tasks into the scenario portion of the test as possible, but maintain the flexibility to change due to unexpected situations as they arise and still result in an efficient and valid test. **Any Task selected for evaluation during a practical test must be evaluated in its entirety.** If the applicant is unable to perform a Task listed in the "plan of action" due to circumstances beyond his/her control, the examiner may substitute another Task from the applicable Area of Operation.

The examiner is not required to follow the precise order in which the Areas of Operation and Tasks appear in this book. The examiner may change the sequence or combine Tasks with similar objectives to have an orderly and efficient flow of the practical test.

The "plan of action" for a test administered **for the addition of an aircraft category and/or class rating** to a flight instructor certificate includes the required Areas of Operation as indicated in the table at the beginning of each section. The required Tasks appropriate to the rating(s) sought must also be included. In some instances, notes identify additional required Tasks. **Any Task selected must be evaluated in its entirety.**

Note: *Area of Operation XI: Slow Flight, Stalls, and Spins, contains Tasks referred to as "proficiency" and "demonstration." The intent of Tasks B and C for single-engine (proficiency) is to ensure that the flight instructor applicant is tested on proficiency for the purpose of teaching students these Tasks that are required for pilot certification. The intent of Tasks D, E, F, and H (demonstration) for single-engine and Task D for multiengine is to ensure that the flight instructor applicant is knowledgeable and proficient in these maneuvers and can teach them to students for both familiarization and stall/spin awareness purposes.*

With the exception of the **required** Tasks, the examiner must not tell the applicant in advance which Tasks will be included in the "plan of action." The applicant should be well prepared in **all** knowledge and skill areas included in the standards. Throughout the flight portion of the practical test, the examiner will evaluate the applicant's ability to simultaneously demonstrate and explain procedures and maneuvers, and to give flight instruction to students at various stages of flight training and levels of experience.

The purpose for including common errors in certain Tasks is to assist the examiner in determining that the flight instructor applicant has the ability to recognize, analyze, and correct such errors. The common errors listed in the Task Objectives may or may not be found in the Task References. However, the FAA considers their frequency of occurrence justification for their inclusion in the Task Objectives.

The examiner is expected to use good judgment in the performance of simulated emergency procedures. The use of the safest means for simulation is expected. Consideration must be given to local conditions, both meteorological and topographical, at the time of the test, as well as the applicant's workload, and the condition of the aircraft used. If the procedure being evaluated would jeopardize safety, it is expected that the applicant will simulate that portion of the maneuver.

Special Emphasis Areas

Examiners must place special emphasis upon areas of aircraft operation considered critical to flight safety. Among these are:

1. Positive aircraft control.
2. Positive exchange of the flight controls procedure.
3. Stall/spin awareness.
4. Collision avoidance.
5. Wake turbulence avoidance.
6. LAHSO.

7. Runway incursion avoidance.
8. CFIT.
9. ADM and risk management.
10. Wire strike avoidance.
11. Checklist usage.
12. Temporary flight restrictions (TFRs).
13. Special use airspace (SUA).
14. Aviation security.
15. Single-Pilot Resource Management (SRM).
16. Other areas deemed appropriate to any phase of the practical test.

With the exception of SRM and the runway incursion avoidance, a given special emphasis area may not be specifically addressed under a given Task. All areas are essential to flight safety and will be evaluated during the practical test.

Practical Test Prerequisites

An applicant for a flight instructor, initial certification practical test is required by 14 CFR part 61 to:

1. Be at least 18 years of age.
2. Be able to read, speak, write, and understand the English language. If there is a doubt, use AC 60-28, English Language Skill Standards.
3. Hold either a commercial/instrument pilot or airline transport pilot certificate with an aircraft category rating appropriate to the flight instructor rating sought.
4. Have an endorsement from an authorized instructor on the fundamentals of instructing appropriate to the required knowledge test.
5. Have passed the appropriate flight instructor knowledge test(s) since the beginning of the 24th month before the month in which he or she takes the practical test. Knowledge test validity can be verified in FAA Order 8080.6, Conduct of Airman Knowledge Tests, Chapter 7, Eligibility Requirements.
6. Have an endorsement from an authorized instructor certifying that the applicant has been given flight training in the Areas of Operation listed in 14 CFR part 61, section 61.187, and a written statement from an authorized flight instructor within the preceding 2 calendar months, in accordance with 14 CFR part 61, section 61.39, that instruction was given in preparation for the practical test. The endorsement must also state that the instructor finds the applicant prepared for the required practical test, and that the applicant has demonstrated satisfactory knowledge

of the subject area(s) in which the applicant was deficient on the airman knowledge test.

An applicant holding a flight instructor certificate who applies for an **additional** rating on that certificate is required by 14 CFR to:

1. Hold a valid pilot certificate with ratings appropriate to the flight instructor rating sought.
2. Have at least 15 hours as pilot in command in the category and class aircraft appropriate to the rating sought.
3. Have passed the appropriate knowledge test prescribed for the issuance of a flight instructor certificate with the rating sought since the beginning of the 24th month before the month in which he/she takes the practical test.
4. Have an endorsement from an authorized instructor certifying that the applicant has been given flight training in the Areas of Operation listed in 14 CFR part 61, section 61.187, and a written statement from an authorized flight instructor within the preceding 2 calendar months, in accordance with 14 CFR part 61, section 61.39, that instruction was given in preparation for the practical test. The endorsement must also state that the instructor finds the applicant prepared for the required practical test, and that the applicant has demonstrated satisfactory knowledge of the subject area(s) in which the applicant was deficient on the airman knowledge test.

If there are questions concerning English language requirements, refer to your local FSDO or to AC 60-28, English Language Skill Standards Required by 14 CFR parts 61, 63, and 65. English language requirements should be determined to be met prior to beginning the practical test.

Aircraft and Equipment Required for the Practical Test

The flight instructor applicant is required by 14 CFR part 61, section 61.45 to provide an airworthy, certificated aircraft for use during the practical test. This section further requires that the aircraft must:

1. Be of U.S., foreign, or military registry of the same category, class, and type for the certificate and/or rating for which the applicant is applying.
2. Have fully functioning dual controls except as provided in 14 CFR part 61, section 61.45(c) and (e).

3. Be capable of performing all appropriate Tasks for the flight instructor rating sought and have no operating limitations, which prohibit the performance of those Tasks.
4. There is no requirement to supply a single-engine complex airplane for the instructor practical test. An applicant may supply a single-engine complex airplane, if desired.

Flight Instructor Responsibility

An appropriately rated flight instructor is responsible for training the flight instructor applicant to acceptable standards in **all** subject matter areas, procedures, and maneuvers included in the Tasks within each Area of Operation in the appropriate flight instructor practical test standard.

Because of the impact of their teaching activities in developing safe, proficient pilots, flight instructors should exhibit a high level of knowledge, skill, and the ability to impart that knowledge and skill to students. The flight instructor must certify that the applicant is:

1. Able to make a practical application of the fundamentals of instructing;

2. Competent to teach the subject matter, procedures, and maneuvers included in the standards to students with varying backgrounds and levels of experience and ability;

3. Able to perform the procedures and maneuvers included in the standards to at least the Commercial Pilot skill level while giving effective flight instruction; and

4. Competent to pass the required practical test for the issuance of the flight instructor certificate with the associated category and class ratings or the addition of a category and/or class rating to a flight instructor certificate.

Throughout the applicant's training, the flight instructor is responsible for emphasizing the performance of, and the ability to teach, **effective visual scanning, runway incursion avoidance, collision avoidance procedures, and Land and Hold Short Operations (LAHSO).** The flight instructor applicant should develop and use scenario-based teaching methods particularly on special emphasis areas. These areas are covered in AC 90-48, "Pilot's Role in Collision Avoidance"; FAA-H-8083-3, "Airplane Flying Handbook"; FAA-H-8083-25, "Pilot's Handbook of Aeronautical Knowledge"; and the current Aeronautical Information Manual.

Examiner Responsibility

The examiner conducting the practical test is responsible for determining that the applicant meets acceptable standards of teaching ability, knowledge, and skill in the selected Tasks. The examiner makes this determination by accomplishing an Objective that is appropriate to each selected Task, and includes an evaluation of the applicant's:

1. Ability to apply the fundamentals of instructing;

2. Knowledge of, and ability to teach, the subject matter, procedures, and maneuvers covered in the Tasks;

3. Ability to perform the procedures and maneuvers included in the standards to the Commercial Pilot skill level while giving effective flight instruction; and

4. Ability to analyze and correct common errors related to the procedures and maneuvers covered in the Tasks.

It is intended that oral questioning be used at any time during the ground or flight portion of the practical test to determine that the applicant can instruct effectively and has a comprehensive knowledge of the Tasks and their related safety factors.

During the flight portion of the practical test, the examiner acts as a student during selected maneuvers. This gives the examiner an opportunity to evaluate the flight instructor applicant's ability to analyze and correct simulated common errors related to these maneuvers. The examiner must place special emphasis on the applicant's use of visual scanning and collision avoidance procedures, and the applicant's ability to teach those procedures.

Examiners should go to the greatest extent possible to test the applicant's application and correlation skills. When possible, scenario-based questions should be used during the practical test. The examiner will evaluate the applicant's ability to teach visual scanning, runway incursion avoidance, collision avoidance procedures, and Land and Hold Short Operations (LAHSO).

If the examiner determines that a Task is incomplete or the outcome uncertain, the examiner may require the applicant to repeat the entire Task or portions of the Task. This provision has been made in the interest of fairness and does not mean that instruction, practice, or the repeating of an unsatisfactory Task is permitted during the certification process. When practical, the remaining Tasks of the practical test phase should be completed before repeating the questionable Task.

On multiengine practical tests, where the failure of the most critical engine after lift off is required, the instructor applicant and examiner must give consideration to local atmospheric conditions, terrain and type of aircraft used. However, the failure of an engine shall not be simulated until attaining at least V_{SSE}/V_{YSE} and at an altitude not lower than 400 feet AGL.

During simulated engine failures on multiengine practical tests, after simulated feathering of the propeller, the engine shall be set to zero thrust. The examiner shall require the instructor applicant to simultaneously demonstrate and explain procedures for landing with a simulated feathered propeller with the engine set to zero thrust. **The examiner must not simulate any conditions that may jeopardize safe flight or result in possible damage to the aircraft.**

Satisfactory Performance

The practical test is passed if, in the judgment of the examiner, the applicant demonstrates satisfactory performance with regard to:

1. Knowledge of the fundamentals of instructing;
2. Knowledge of the technical subject areas;
3. Knowledge of the flight instructor's responsibilities concerning the pilot certification process;
4. Knowledge of the flight instructor's responsibilities concerning logbook entries and pilot certificate endorsements;
5. Knowledge of the flight instructor's responsibilities conveying to the applicant runway incursion mitigation techniques and procedures.

6. Ability to demonstrate the procedures and maneuvers selected by the examiner to at least the Commercial Pilot skill level while giving effective instruction;
7. Competence in teaching the procedures and maneuvers selected by the examiner;
8. Competence in describing, recognizing, analyzing, and correcting common errors simulated by the examiner; and
9. Knowledge of the development and effective use of a course of training, a syllabus, and a lesson plan.

Unsatisfactory Performance

If, in the judgment of the examiner, the applicant does not meet the standards of performance on any of the Tasks performed, the applicable Area of Operation is considered unsatisfactory and therefore, the practical test is failed. The examiner or applicant may discontinue the test at any time when the failure of an Area of Operation makes the applicant ineligible for the certificate or rating sought. **The test is continued only with the consent of the applicant.** If the test is discontinued, the applicant is entitled credit for only those Areas of Operation and their associated Tasks satisfactorily performed; however, during the retest and at the discretion of the examiner, any Task may be reevaluated, including those previously considered satisfactory. Specific reasons for disqualification are:

1. Failure to perform a procedure or maneuver to the Commercial Pilot skill level while giving effective flight instruction;
2. Failure to provide an effective instructional explanation while demonstrating a procedure or maneuver (explanation during the demonstration must be clear, concise, technically accurate, and complete with no prompting from the examiner);
3. Any action or lack of action by the applicant which requires corrective intervention by the examiner to maintain safe flight;
4. Failure to use proper and effective visual scanning techniques to clear the area before and while performing maneuvers.

When a Disapproval Notice is issued, the examiner must record the applicant's unsatisfactory performance in terms of Areas of Operation and specific Tasks not meeting the standard appropriate to the practical test conducted. If the applicant fails the practical test because of a special emphasis area, the Notice of Disapproval must indicate the associated Task. An example would be: "Area of Operation IX: Maneuvering during Slow Flight, failure to teach proper collision avoidance procedures."

Letter of Discontinuance

When a practical test is discontinued for reasons other than unsatisfactory performance (e.g., equipment failure, weather, or illness), FAA Form 8700-1, Airman Certificate and/or Rating Application, and, if applicable, the Airman Knowledge Test Report, is to be returned to the applicant. The examiner, at that time, is to prepare, sign, and issue a Letter of Discontinuance to the applicant. The Letter of Discontinuance should identify the Areas of Operation and their associated Tasks of the practical test that were successfully completed. The applicant should be advised that the Letter of Discontinuance must be presented to the examiner when the practical test is resumed and made part of the certification file.

Aeronautical Decision Making and Risk Management

Throughout the practical test, the examiner will evaluate the applicant's ability to use good aeronautical decision making procedures in order to identify risks. The examiner will accomplish this requirement by developing scenarios that incorporate as many Tasks as possible to evaluate the applicants risk management in making safe aeronautical decisions. For example, the examiner may develop a scenario that incorporates weather decisions and performance planning, and distractions that may result in a loss of runway/taxiway situational awareness (e.g. ATC communications congestion, accomplishing checklist procedures, talking with passengers, cell phone/texting during taxiing, etc).

The applicant's ability to utilize all the assets available in making a risk analysis to determine the safest course of action is essential for satisfactory performance. The scenarios should be realistic and within the capabilities of the aircraft used for the practical test.

Single-Pilot Resource Management

Single-Pilot Resource Management refers to the effective use of **all** available resources: human resources, hardware, and information. It is similar to Crew Resource Management (CRM) procedures that are being emphasized in multi-crewmember operations except that only one crewmember (the pilot) is involved. Human resources "...includes all other groups routinely working with the pilot who are involved in decisions that are required to operate a flight safely. These groups include, but are not limited to dispatchers, weather briefers, maintenance personnel, and air traffic controllers." Pilot Resource Management is not a single Task; it is a set of skill competencies that must be evident in all Tasks in this practical test standard as applied to single-pilot operation.

Applicant's Use of Checklists

Throughout the practical test, the instructor applicant is evaluated on the use and teaching of an appropriate checklist. Proper use is dependent on the specific Task being evaluated. The situation may be such that the use of the checklist, while accomplishing elements of an Objective, would be either unsafe or impractical, especially in a single-pilot operation. In this case, a review of the checklist after the elements have been accomplished would be appropriate.

Use of Distractions during Practical Tests

Numerous studies indicate that many accidents and runway incursions have occurred when the pilot has been distracted during taxi operations and critical phases of flight. To evaluate the applicant's ability to utilize proper control technique while dividing attention both inside and outside the cockpit, the examiner must cause realistic distractions during ground operations and use the flight portion of the practical test to evaluate the applicant's ability to divide attention while maintaining safe operation while on the ground and in flight.

Positive Exchange of Flight Controls

During flight training, there must always be a clear understanding between students and flight instructors of who has control of the aircraft. Prior to flight, a briefing should be conducted that includes the procedure for the exchange of flight controls. A positive three-step process in the exchange of flight controls between pilots is a proven procedure and one that is strongly recommended.

When the instructor wishes the student to take control of the aircraft, he or she will say, "You have the flight controls." The student will acknowledge immediately by saying, "I have the flight controls." The flight instructor will again say, "You have the flight controls." When control is returned to the instructor, the same procedure will be followed. A visual check is recommended to verify that the exchange has occurred. There should never be any doubt as to who is flying the aircraft. The instructor applicant is expected to teach proper positive exchange of flight controls during the practical test.

Initial Flight Instructor Certification

An applicant who seeks initial flight instructor certification will be evaluated in all Areas of Operation of the standards appropriate to the rating(s) sought. The examiner must refer to the Note in the front of the Area of Operation to determine which Tasks to test.

Addition of Aircraft Category and/or Class Ratings to a Flight Instructor Certificate

An applicant who holds a flight instructor certificate and seeks an additional aircraft category and/or class rating will be evaluated in the runway incursion avoidance Task and at least the Areas of Operation and Tasks that are unique and appropriate to the rating(s) sought (see table at the beginning of each section). At the discretion of the examiner, the applicant's competence in **all** Areas of Operation may be evaluated.

Renewal or Reinstatement of a Flight Instructor Certificate

14 CFR part 61, sections 61.197(a)(1) and 61.199(a), allows an individual that holds a flight instructor certificate to renew or reinstate that certificate by passing a practical test. The examiner shall develop a plan of action that includes the Areas of Operation and at least the minimum number of Tasks prescribed in the table at the beginning of each section and the runway incursion avoidance Task. The Renewal or Reinstatement of one rating on a Flight Instructor Certificate renews or reinstates all privileges existing on the certificate.

(this page intentionally left blank)

Section 1:

Flight Instructor – Airplane

Single-Engine

(this page intentionally left blank)

Additional Rating Task Table: Single-Engine Airplane

Addition of a single-engine class rating (and an airplane category rating, if appropriate) to a flight instructor certificate.

Flight Instructor Certificate and Rating(s) Held

Required Area of Operation	AME	RH	RG	G	IA	IH
I	None	None	None	None	None	None
II	B,M	B,D,E, M	B,D,E, M	B,D,E, M	*	*
III	None	C,D	C,D	C,D	All	All
IV	None	None	None	None	None	None
V	None	*	*	*	*	*
VI	None	*	None	*	*	*
VII	*	*	*	*	*	*
VIII	None	*	*	*	*	*
IX	*	*	*	*	*	*
X	D	*	*	*	*	*
XI	*	*	*	*	*	*
XII	None	*	*	*	None	*
XIII	*	*	*	*	*	*
XIV	None	*	*	*	*	*

*Refer to the Note under the respective Area of Operation for Task requirements.

Note: If an applicant holds more than one rating on a flight instructor certificate and the table indicates both a "None" and a "Select One" for a particular Area of Operation, the "None" entry applies. This is logical since the applicant has satisfactorily accomplished the Area of Operation on a previous flight instructor practical test. At the discretion of the examiner, the applicant's competence in **any** Area of Operation may be evaluated.

Renewal or Reinstatement of a Flight Instructor Table: Airplane Single-Engine Category

Required Area of Operation	Number of Tasks
II	Task B, M, and 1 other Task
III	1
IV	1
V	1
VII	2 Takeoffs and 2 Landings
IX	1
X	1
XI	2
XIII	1
XIV	1

The Renewal or Reinstatement of one rating on a Flight Instructor Certificate renews or reinstates all privileges existing on the certificate. (14 CFR part 61, section 61.197 and section 61.199)

Applicant's Practical Test Checklist

Appointment with Inspector or Examiner

Name: _____

Date/Time: _____

ACCEPTABLE AIRCRAFT

- ☐ View-Limiting Device (if applicable)
- ☐ Aircraft Documents:
    - ☐ Airworthiness Certificate
    - ☐ Registration Certificate
    - ☐ Operating Limitations
- ☐ Aircraft Maintenance Records:
    - ☐ Airworthiness Inspections
- ☐ Pilot's Operating Handbook and FAA-Approved Airplane Flight Manual

PERSONAL EQUIPMENT

- ☐ Current Aeronautical Charts
- ☐ Computer and Plotter
- ☐ Flight Plan Form
- ☐ Flight Logs
- ☐ Current AIM
- ☐ Current Airport/Facility Directory

PERSONAL RECORDS

- ☐ Pilot Certificate
- ☐ Medical Certificate
- ☐ Completed FAA Form 8710-1, Airman Certificate and/or Rating Application
- ☐ Airman Knowledge Test Report
- ☐ Logbook with Instructor's Endorsement
- ☐ Letter of Discontinuance (if applicable)
- ☐ Notice of Disapproval (if applicable)
- ☐ Approved School Graduation Certificate (if applicable)
- ☐ Examiner's Fee (if applicable)

FAA-S-8081-6D

(this page intentionally left blank)

Examiner's Practical Test Checklist

Flight Instructor – Airplane

(Single-Engine)

Applicant's Name: _____

Examiner's Name: _____

Date: _____ **Type Check:** _____

Type Airplane: _____

Area of Operation:

I. FUNDAMENTALS OF INSTRUCTING
- ☐ **A.** Human Behavior and Effective Communication
- ☐ **B.** The Learning Process
- ☐ **C.** The Teaching Process
- ☐ **D.** Assessment and Critique
- ☐ **E.** Instructor Responsibilities and Professionalism
- ☐ **F.** Techniques of Flight Instruction
- ☐ **G.** Risk Management

II. TECHNICAL SUBJECT AREAS
- ☐ **A.** Aeromedical Factors
- ☐ **B.** Runway Incursion Avoidance
- ☐ **C.** Visual Scanning and Collision Avoidance
- ☐ **D.** Principles of Flight
- ☐ **E.** Airplane Flight Controls
- ☐ **F.** Airplane Weight and Balance
- ☐ **G.** Navigation and Flight Planning
- ☐ **H.** Night Operations
- ☐ **I.** High Altitude Operations
- ☐ **J.** 14 CFR and Publications
- ☐ **K.** National Airspace System
- ☐ **L.** Navigation Systems and Radar Services
- ☐ **M.** Logbook Entries and Certificate Endorsements
- ☐ **N.** Water and Seaplane Characteristics
- ☐ **O.** Seaplane Bases, Rules, and Aids to Marine Navigation

III. PREFLIGHT PREPARATION
- ☐ **A.** Certificates and Documents
- ☐ **B.** Weather Information
- ☐ **C.** Operation of Systems
- ☐ **D.** Performance and Limitations

    ☐   **E.** Airworthiness Requirements

IV. PREFLIGHT LESSON ON A MANEUVER TO BE PERFORMED IN FLIGHT

    ☐   **A.** Maneuver Lesson

V. PREFLIGHT PROCEDURES

    ☐   **A.** Preflight Inspection
    ☐   **B.** Cockpit Management
    ☐   **C.** Engine Starting
    ☐   **D.** Taxiing—Landplane
    ☐   **E.** Taxiing—Seaplane
    ☐   **F.** Sailing
    ☐   **G.** Before Takeoff Check

VI. AIRPORT AND SEAPLANE BASE OPERATIONS

    ☐   **A.** Radio Communications and ATC Light Signals
    ☐   **B.** Traffic Patterns
    ☐   **C.** Airport/Seaplane Base, Runway and Taxiway Signs, Markings, and Lighting

VII. TAKEOFFS, LANDINGS, AND GO-AROUNDS

    ☐   **A.** Normal and Crosswind Takeoff and Climb
    ☐   **B.** Short-Field (Confined Area ASES) Takeoff and Maximum Performance Climb
    ☐   **C.** Soft-Field Takeoff and Climb
    ☐   **D.** Glassy-Water Takeoff and Climb
    ☐   **E.** Rough-Water Takeoff and Climb
    ☐   **F.** Normal and Crosswind Approach and Landing
    ☐   **G.** Slip to a Landing
    ☐   **H.** Go-Around/Rejected Landing
    ☐   **I.** Short-Field (Confined Area ASES) Approach and Landing
    ☐   **J.** Soft-Field Approach and Landing
    ☐   **K.** Power-Off 180° Accuracy Approach and Landing
    ☐   **L.** Glassy-Water Approach and Landing
    ☐   **M.** Rough-Water Approach and Landing

VIII. FUNDAMENTALS OF FLIGHT

    ☐   **A.** Straight-and-Level Flight
    ☐   **B.** Level Turns
    ☐   **C.** Straight Climbs and Climbing Turns
    ☐   **D.** Straight Descents and Descending Turns

IX. PERFORMANCE MANEUVERS

    ☐   **A.** Steep Turns
    ☐   **B.** Steep Spirals
    ☐   **C.** Chandelles

☐ **D.** Lazy Eights

X. GROUND REFERENCE MANEUVERS

☐ **A.** Rectangular Course

☐ **B.** S-Turns Across a Road

☐ **C.** Turns Around a Point

☐ **D.** Eights on Pylons

XI. SLOW FLIGHT, STALLS, AND SPINS

☐ **A.** Maneuvering During Slow Flight

☐ **B.** Power-On Stalls (Proficiency)

☐ **C.** Power-Off Stalls (Proficiency)

☐ **D.** Cross-controlled Stalls (Demonstration)

☐ **E.** Elevator Trim Stalls (Demonstration)

☐ **F.** Secondary Stalls (Demonstration)

☐ **G.** Spins

☐ **H.** Accelerated Maneuver Stalls (Demonstration)

XII. BASIC INSTRUMENT MANEUVERS

☐ **A.** Straight-and-Level Flight

☐ **B.** Constant Airspeed Climbs

☐ **C.** Constant Airspeed Descents

☐ **D.** Turns to Headings

☐ **E.** Recovery from Unusual Flight Attitudes

XIII. EMERGENCY OPERATIONS

☐ **A.** Emergency Approach and Landing (Simulated)

☐ **B.** Systems and Equipment Malfunctions

☐ **C.** Emergency Equipment and Survival Gear

☐ **D.** Emergency Descent

XIV. POSTFLIGHT PROCEDURES

☐ **A.** Postflight Procedures

☐ **B.** Anchoring

☐ **C.** Docking and Mooring

☐ **D.** Beaching

☐ **E.** Ramping

(this page intentionally left blank)

Areas of Operation:

I.   Fundamentals of Instructing

Note: *The examiner shall select Task E and one other Task.*

Task A: *Human Behavior and Effective Communication*

Reference: *FAA-H-8083-9A.*

Objective: To determine that the applicant exhibits instructional knowledge of human behavior and effective communication and how these impact effective learning by describing:

1.   Definitions of human behavior.
2.   Human needs and motivation.
3.   Defense mechanisms.
4.   Student emotional reactions.
5.   Basic elements of communication.
6.   Barriers to effective communication.
7.   Developing communication skills.

Task B: *The Learning Process*

Reference: *FAA-H-8083-9A.*

Objective: To determine that the applicant exhibits instructional knowledge of the learning process by describing:

1.   Learning theory.
2.   Perceptions and insight.
3.   Acquiring knowledge.
4.   The laws of learning.
5.   Domains of learning.
6.   Characteristics of learning.
7.   Acquiring skill knowledge.
8.   Types of practice.
9.   Scenario-based training.
10.   Errors.
11.   Memory and forgetting.
12.   Retention of learning.
13.   Transfer of learning.

Task C: The Teaching Process

Reference: *FAA-H-8083-9A.*

Objective: To determine that the applicant exhibits instructional knowledge of the teaching process by describing:

1. Preparation of a lesson.
2. Organization of material.
3. Training delivery methods:

    a. Lecture method.
    b. Guided discussion method.
    c. Computer-assisted learning method.
    d. Demonstration-performance method.
    e. Drill and practice method.

4. Problem based learning.
5. Instruction aids and training technologies.

Task D: Assessment and Critique

Reference: *FAA-H-8083-9A.*

Objective: To determine that the applicant exhibits instructional knowledge of assessments and critiques by describing:

1. Assessment:

    a. Purpose of assessment.
    b. General characteristics of effective assessment.
    c. Traditional assessment.
    d. Authentic assessment.
    e. Oral assessment.
    f. Characteristics of effective questions.
    g. Types of questions to avoid.

2. Critique:

    a. Instructors/student critique.
    b. Student-lead critique.
    c. Small group critique.
    d. Individual student critique by another student.
    e. Self-critique.
    f. Written critique.

Task E: Instructor Responsibilities and Professionalism

Reference: *FAA-H-8083-9A.*

Objective: To determine that the applicant exhibits instructional knowledge of instructor responsibilities and professionalism by describing:

1. Aviation instructor responsibilities:

   a. Helping students learn.
   b. Providing adequate instruction.
   c. Standards of performance.
   d. Minimizing student frustrations.

2. Flight instructor responsibilities:

   a. Physiological obstacles for flight students.
   b. Ensuring student ability.

3. Professionalism.
4. Evaluation of student ability.
5. Aviation instructors and exams.
6. Professional development.

Task F: Techniques of Flight Instruction

Reference: *FAA-H-8083-9A.*

Objective: To determine that the applicant exhibits instructional knowledge of instructor responsibilities and professionalism by describing:

1. Obstacles in learning during flight instruction.
2. Demonstration-performance training delivery.
3. Positive exchange of controls.
4. Sterile cockpit.
5. Use of distractions.
6. Integrated flight instruction.
7. Assessment of piloting ability.
8. Aeronautical decision making.

Task G: Risk Management

References: *FAA-H-8083-9A, FAA-H-8083-2*

Objective: To determine that the applicant exhibits instructional knowledge of risk management by describing:

1. Principles of risk management.
2. Risk management process.
3. Level of risk.
4. Assessing risk.
5. Mitigating risk.
6. IMSAFE checklist.

7. PAVE checklist.
8. 5P checklist.

II.   Technical Subject Areas

Note: The examiner must select Tasks B, M, and at least one
              other Task.

Task A: Aeromedical Factors

References: AIM; FAA-H-8083-3, FAA-S-8081-12, FAA-S-ACS-6.

Objective: To determine that the applicant exhibits instructional
                  knowledge of the elements related to aeromedical
                  factors by describing:

1.   How to obtain an appropriate medical certificate.
2.   How to obtain a medical certificate in the event of a
     possible medical deficiency.
3.   The causes, symptoms, effects, and corrective action of the
     following medical factors:

   a.   Hypoxia
   b.   Hyperventilation
   c.   Middle ear and sinus problems
   d.   Spatial disorientation
   e.   Motion sickness
   f.   Carbon monoxide poisoning
   g.   Fatigue and stress
   h.   Dehydration

4.   The effects of alcohol and drugs, and their relationship to
     flight safety.
5.   The effect of nitrogen excesses incurred during scuba dives
     and how this affects pilots and passengers during flight.

Task B: Runway Incursion Avoidance

*References: AC 91-73, A/FD, AIM; FAA-H-8083-2, FAA-H-8083-3,
             FAA-H-8083-25.*

Note: If this task has been previously performed in the aircraft
              during an earlier instructor rating, the determination of the
              required knowledge can be demonstrated during the brief,
              at the discretion of the examiner.

Objective: To determine that the applicant exhibits instructional
                  knowledge of the elements of runway incursion
                  avoidance by describing:

1.   Distinct challenges and requirements during taxi operations
     not found in other phases of flight operations.

2. Procedures for appropriate cockpit activities during taxiing including taxi route planning, briefing the location of hot spots, communicating and coordinating with ATC.
3. Procedures for steering, maneuvering, maintaining taxiway, runway position, and situational awareness.
4. The relevance/importance of hold lines.
5. Procedures for ensuring the pilot maintains strict focus on the movement of the aircraft and ATC communications, including the elimination of all distractive activities (i.e. cell phone, texting, conversations with passengers) during aircraft taxi, takeoff and climb out to cruise altitude.
6. Procedures for holding the pilot's workload to a minimum during taxi operations which should increase the pilot's awareness while taxiing.
7. Taxi operation planning procedures, such as recording taxi instructions, reading back taxi clearances, and reviewing taxi routes on the airport diagram,
8. Procedures for ensuring that clearance or instructions that are actually received are adhered to rather than the ones expected to be received.
9. Procedures for maintaining/enhancing situational awareness when conducting taxi operations in relation to other aircraft operations in the vicinity as well as to other vehicles moving on the airport.
10. Procedures for briefing if a landing rollout to a taxiway exit will place the pilot in close proximity to another runway which can result in a runway incursion.
11. Appropriate after landing/taxi procedures in the event the aircraft is on a taxiway that is between parallel runways.
12. Specific procedures for operations at an airport with an operating air traffic control tower, with emphasis on ATC communications and runway entry/crossing authorizations.
13. ATC communications and pilot actions before takeoff, before landing, and after landing at towered and non-towered airports.
14. Procedures unique to night operations.
15. Operations at non-towered airports.
16. Use of aircraft exterior lighting.
17. Low visibility operations.

Task C: *Visual Scanning and Collision Avoidance*

References: AC 90-48; AIM; FAA-H-8083-3, FAA-H-8083-25.

Objective: To determine that the applicant exhibits instructional knowledge of the elements of visual scanning and collision avoidance by describing:

1. Relationship between a pilot's physical condition and vision.
2. Environmental conditions that degrade vision.

3.   Vestibular and visual illusions.
4.   "See and avoid" concept.
5.   Proper visual scanning procedure.
6.   Relationship between poor visual scanning habits and increased collision risk.
7.   Proper clearing procedures.
8.   Importance of knowing aircraft blind spots.
9.   Relationship between aircraft speed differential and collision risk.
10.   Situations that involve the greatest collision risk.

Task D: Principles of Flight

References: FAA-H-8083-3, FAA-H-8083-25.

Objective: To determine that the applicant exhibits instructional knowledge of the elements of principles of flight by describing:

1.   Airfoil design characteristics.
2.   Airplane stability and controllability.
3.   Turning tendency (torque effect).
4.   Load factors in airplane design.
5.   Wingtip vortices and precautions to be taken.

Task E: Airplane Flight Controls

References: FAA-H-8083-3, FAA-H-8083-25.

Objective: To determine that the applicant exhibits instructional knowledge of the elements related to the airplane flight controls by describing the purpose, location, direction of movement, effect, and proper procedure for use of the:

1.   Primary flight controls.
2.   Secondary flight controls.
3.   Trim Controls.

Task F: Airplane Weight and Balance

References: FAA-H-8083-1, FAA-H-8083-3, FAA-H-8083-25.

Objective: To determine that the applicant exhibits instructional knowledge of the elements of airplane weight and balance by describing:

1.   Weight and balance terms.
2.   Effect of weight and balance on performance.
3.   Methods of weight and balance control.

4. Determination of total weight and center of gravity and the changes that occur when adding, removing, or shifting weight.

Task G: Navigation and Flight Planning

References: FAA-H-8083-3, FAA-H-8083-25.

Objective: To determine that the applicant exhibits instructional knowledge of the elements of navigation and flight planning by describing:

1. Terms used in navigation.
2. Features of aeronautical charts.
3. Importance of using the proper and current aeronautical charts.
4. Method of plotting a course, selection of fuel stops and alternates, and appropriate actions in the event of unforeseen situations.
5. Fundamentals of pilotage and dead reckoning.
6. Fundamentals of radio navigation.
7. Diversion to an alternate.
8. Lost procedures.
9. Computation of fuel consumption.
10. Importance of preparing and properly using a flight log.
11. Importance of a weather check and the use of good judgment in making a "go/no-go" decision.
12. Purpose of and procedure used in filing a flight plan.

Task H: Night Operations

References: AIM; FAA-H-8083-3, FAA-H-8083-25, FAA-S-8081-12, FAA-S-ACS-6.

Objective: To determine that the applicant exhibits instructional knowledge of the elements of night operations by describing:

1. Factors related to night vision.
2. Disorientation and night optical illusions.
3. Proper adjustment of interior lights.
4. Importance of having a flashlight with a red lens.
5. Night preflight inspection.
6. Engine starting procedures, including use of position and anti-collision lights prior to start.
7. Taxiing and orientation on an airport.
8. Takeoff and climb-out.
9. In-flight orientation.
10. Importance of verifying the airplane's attitude by reference to flight instruments.

11. Night emergencies procedures.
12. Traffic patterns.
13. Approaches and landings with and without landing lights.
14. Go-around.

Task I: High Altitude Operations

References: *14 CFR part 91, AC 61-107, AIM, POH/AFM; FAA-H-8083-3, FAA-S-8081-12.*

Objective: To determine that the applicant exhibits instructional knowledge of the elements of high altitude operations by describing:

1. Regulatory requirements for use of oxygen.
2. Physiological hazards associated with high altitude operations.
3. Characteristics of a pressurized airplane and various types of supplemental oxygen systems.
4. Importance of "aviator's breathing oxygen."
5. Care and storage of high-pressure oxygen bottles.
6. Problems associated with rapid decompression and corresponding solutions.
7. Fundamental concept of cabin pressurization.
8. Operation of a cabin pressurization system.

Task J: 14 CFR and Publications

References: *14 CFR parts 1, 61, 91; AC 00-2, AIM, FAA-H-8083-25, NTSB part 830, POH/AFM.*

Objective: To determine that the applicant exhibits instructional knowledge of the elements related to the Code of Federal Regulations and related publications by describing:

1. Availability and method of revision of 14 CFR parts 1, 61, 91, and NTSB part 830 by describing:

   a. Purpose
   b. general content

2. Availability of flight information publications, advisory circulars, practical test standards, pilot operating handbooks, and FAA-approved airplane flight manuals by describing:

   a. Availability.

b. Purpose.
c. General content.

Task K: National Airspace System

References: 14 CFR part 91, AIM; FAA-S-8081-12, FAA-S-ACS-6.

Objective: To determine that the applicant exhibits instructional knowledge of the elements of the national airspace system by describing:

1. Basic VFR Weather Minimums for all classes of airspace.
2. Airspace classes—the operating rules, pilot certification, and airplane equipment requirements for the following:

    a. Class A.
    b. Class B.
    c. Class C.
    d. Class D.
    e. Class E.
    f. Class G.

3. Special use airspace (SUA).
4. Temporary flight restrictions (TFR).

Task L: Navigation Systems and Radar Services

References: AIM; FAA-H-8083-3, FAA-H-8083-15, FAA-S-8081-12, FAA-S-ACS-6.

Objective: To determine that the applicant exhibits instructional knowledge of the elements related to navigation systems and radar service by describing:

1. One ground-based navigational system (VOR/VORTAC, NDB, and DME).
2. Satellite-based navigation system.
3. Radar service and procedures.
4. Global positioning system (GPS).

Task M: Logbook Entries and Certificate Endorsements

References: 14 CFR part 61, AC 61-65.

Objective: To determine that the applicant exhibits instructional knowledge of the elements related to logbook entries and certificate endorsements by describing:

1. Required logbook entries for instruction given.

2. Required student pilot certificate endorsements, including appropriate logbook entries.
3. Preparation of a recommendation for a pilot practical test, including appropriate logbook entry for:

   a. Initial pilot certification.
   b. Additional pilot certification.
   c. Additional aircraft qualification.

4. Required endorsement of a pilot logbook for the satisfactory completion of the required FAA flight review.
5. Required flight instructor records.

Task N: Water and Seaplane Characteristics (ASES)

References: *FAA-H-8083-3, FAA-H-8083-23, FAA-S-8081-12, FAA-S-ACS-6; POH/AFM.*

Objective: To determine that the applicant exhibits instructional knowledge of the elements related to water and seaplane characteristics by describing:

1. The characteristics of water surface as affected by features, such as:

   a. Size and location of water operating area.
   b. Protected and unprotected operating areas.
   c. Surface wind.
   d. Direction and height of waves.
   e. Direction and strength of water current.
   f. Floating and partially submerged debris.
   g. Sandbars, islands, and shoals.

2. Seaplane's float or hull construction and its relationship to performance.
3. Causes of porpoising and skipping and pilot action necessary to prevent or correct those occurrences.

Task O: Seaplane Bases, Rules, and Aids to Marine Navigation (ASES)

References: *14 CFR part 91, COMDTINST; FAA-H-8083-3, FAA-H-8083-23, FAA-S-8081-12, FAA-S-ACS-6; M16672.2D.*

Objective: To determine that the applicant exhibits instructional knowledge of the elements related to seaplane bases, rules, and aids to marine navigation by describing:

1. How to locate and identify seaplane bases on charts or in directories.

2. Operating restrictions at various seaplane bases.
3. Right-of-way, steering, and sailing rules pertinent to seaplane operation.
4. Purpose and identification of marine navigation aids such as buoys, beacons, lights, and sound signals.

III. Preflight Preparation

Note: *The examiner must select at least one Task.*

Task A: Certificates and Documents

References: *14 CFR parts 23, 43, 61, 67, 91; FAA-H-8083-3, FAA-H-8083-25, FAA-S-8081-12, FAA-S-ACS-6; POH/AFM.*

Objective To determine that the applicant exhibits instructional knowledge of the elements related to certificates and documents by describing:

1. The training requirements for the issuance of a recreational, private, and commercial pilot certificate.
2. The privileges and limitations of pilot certificates and ratings at recreational, private, and commercial levels.
3. Class and duration of medical certificates.
4. Recent pilot flight experience requirements.
5. Required entries in pilot logbook or flight record.

Task B: Weather Information

References: *AC 00-6, AC 00-45; FAA-H-8083-25, FAA-S-8081-12, FAA-S-ACS-6.*

Objective: To determine that the applicant exhibits instructional knowledge of the elements related to weather information by describing:

1. Importance of a thorough preflight weather briefing.
2. Various means and sources of obtaining weather information.
3. Use of real-time weather reports, forecasts, and charts for developing scenario-based training.
4. In-flight weather advisories.
5. Recognition of aviation weather hazards to include wind shear.
6. Factors to be considered in making a "go/no-go" decision.

Task C: Operation of Systems

References: *FAA-H-8083-3, FAA-H-8083-23, FAA-H-8083-25, FAA-S-8081-12, FAA-S-ACS-6; POH/AFM.*

Objective: To determine that the applicant exhibits instructional knowledge of the elements related to the operation of systems, as applicable to the airplane used for the practical test, by describing the following systems:

1. Primary and secondary flight controls
2. Trim
3. Water rudders (ASES)
4. Powerplant and propeller
5. Landing gear
6. Fuel, oil, and hydraulic
7. Electrical
8. Avionics including autopilot
9. Pitot static, vacuum/pressure and associated instruments
10. Environmental
11. Deicing and anti-icing

Task D: *Performance and Limitations*

References: *AC 61-84; FAA-H-8083-3, FAA-H-8083-23,*
FAA-H-8083-25, FAA-S-8081-12, FAA-S-ACS-6;
POH/AFM.

Objective: To determine that the applicant exhibits instructional
knowledge of the elements related to performance
and limitations by describing:

1. Determination of weight and balance condition.
2. Use of performance charts, tables, and other data in
determining performance in various phases of flight.
3. Effects of exceeding airplane limitations.
4. Effects of atmospheric conditions on performance.
5. Factors to be considered in determining that the required
performance is within the airplane's capabilities.

Task E: *Airworthiness Requirements*

References: *14 CFR parts 23, 39, 43; FAA-S-8081-12,*
FAA-S-ACS-6; POH/AFM.

Objective: To determine that the applicant exhibits instructional
knowledge of the elements related to required
airworthiness by explaining:

1. Required instruments and equipment for day/night VFR.
2. Procedures and limitations for determining airworthiness of
the airplane with inoperative instruments and equipment
with and without a minimum equipment list (MEL).
3. Requirements and procedures for obtaining a special flight
permit.
4. Airworthiness directives, compliance records, maintenance/
inspection requirements, and appropriate records.
5. Procedures for deferring maintenance on aircraft without an
approved MEL.

IV. Preflight Lesson on a Maneuver to be Performed in Flight

Note: *Examiner must select at least one maneuver Task from Areas of Operation VII through XIII, and ask the applicant to present a preflight lesson on the selected maneuver as the lesson would be taught to a student.*

Task A: Maneuver Lesson

References: *FAA-H-8083-3, FAA-H-8083-9, FAA-H-8083-23, FAA-H-8083-25, FAA-S-8081-12, FAA-S-ACS-6; POH/AFM.*

Objective: To determine that the applicant exhibits instructional knowledge of the selected maneuver by:

1. Stating the purpose.
2. Giving an accurate, comprehensive oral description, including the elements and common errors.
3. Using instructional aids, as appropriate.
4. Describing the recognition, analysis, and correction of common errors.

V. Preflight Procedures

Note: *The examiner must select at least one Task.*

Task A: *Preflight Inspection (ASEL and ASES)*

References: *AC 61-84; FAA-H-8083-3, FAA-H-8083-23, FAA-S-8081-12, FAA-S-ACS-6; POH/AFM.*

Objective: To determine that the applicant:

1. Exhibits instructional knowledge of the elements of a preflight inspection, as applicable to the airplane used for the practical test, by describing:

   a. Reasons for the preflight inspection, items that should be inspected, and how defects are detected.
   b. Importance of using the appropriate checklist.
   c. How to determine fuel and oil quantity and contamination.
   d. Detection of fuel, oil, and hydraulic leaks.
   e. Inspection of the oxygen system, including supply and proper operation (if applicable).
   f. Inspection of the flight controls and water rudder (if applicable).
   g. Detection of visible structural damage.
   h. Removal of tie-downs, control locks, and wheel chocks.
   i. Removal of ice and frost.
   j. Importance of the proper loading and securing of baggage, cargo, and equipment.
   k. Use of sound judgment in determining whether the airplane is airworthy and in condition for safe flight.

2. Exhibits instructional knowledge of common errors related to a preflight inspection by describing:

   a. Failure to use or the improper use of checklist.
   b. Hazards which may result from allowing distractions to interrupt a visual inspection.
   c. Inability to recognize discrepancies to determine airworthiness.
   d. Failure to ensure servicing with the proper fuel and oil.
   e. Failure to ensure proper loading and securing of baggage, cargo, and equipment.

3. Demonstrates and simultaneously explains a preflight inspection from an instructional standpoint.

Task B: Cockpit Management (ASEL and ASES)

References: FAA-H-8083-3, FAA-S-8081-12; POH/AFM.

Objective: To determine that the applicant:

1. Exhibits instructional knowledge of the elements of cockpit management by describing:

    a. Proper arranging and securing of essential materials and equipment in the cockpit.
    b. Proper use and/or adjustment of cockpit items such as safety belts, shoulder harnesses, rudder pedals, and seats.
    c. Occupant briefing on emergency procedures and use of safety belts.
    d. Proper utilization of all resources required to operate a flight safely: dispatchers, weather briefers, maintenance personnel, and air traffic control.

2. Exhibits instructional knowledge of common errors related to cockpit management by describing:

    a. Failure to place and secure essential materials and equipment for easy access during flight.
    b. Failure to properly adjust cockpit items, such as safety belts, shoulder harnesses, rudder pedals, and seats.
    c. Failure to provide proper adjustment of equipment and controls.
    d. Failure to provide occupant briefing on emergency procedures and use of safety belts.
    e. Failure to utilize all resources required to operate a flight safely.

3. Demonstrates and simultaneously explains cockpit management from an instructional standpoint.

Task C: Engine Starting (ASEL and ASES)

References: AC 91-13, AC 91-55; FAA-S-8081-12, FAA-S-ACS-6, FAA-H-8083-3, FAA-H-8083-23, FAA-H-8083-25; POH/AFM.

Objective: To determine that the applicant:

1. Exhibits instructional knowledge of the elements of engine starting, as appropriate to the airplane used for the practical test, by describing:

    a. Safety precautions related to starting.
    b. Use of external power.

     c.   Effect of atmospheric conditions on starting.
     d.   Importance of following the appropriate checklist.
     e.   Adjustment of engine controls during start.
     f.   Prevention of airplane movement during and after start.
     g.   Safety procedures for hand-propping an airplane.

2.   Exhibits instructional knowledge of common errors related to engine starting by describing:

     a.   Failure to properly use the appropriate checklist.
     b.   Failure to use safety precautions related to starting.
     c.   Improper adjustment of engine controls during start.
     d.   Failure to assure proper clearance of the propeller.

3.   Demonstrates and simultaneously explains engine starting from an instructional standpoint.

Task D: *Taxiing—Landplane (ASEL)*

References: FAA-H-8083-3, FAA-S-8081-12, FAA-S-ACS-6; POH/AFM.

Objective: To determine that the applicant:

1.   Exhibits instructional knowledge of the elements of landplane taxiing by describing:

     a.   Proper brake check and correct use of brakes.
     b.   Compliance with airport/taxiway surface marking, signals, and ATC clearances or instructions.
     c.   How to control direction and speed.
     d.   Flight control positioning for various wind conditions.
     e.   Procedures used to avoid other aircraft and hazards.
     f.   Runway incursion avoidance procedures.
     g.   Procedures for eliminating pilot distractions.
     h.   Use of taxi chart during taxi.
     i.   Airport, taxiway, and runway position situational awareness.
     j.   Additional taxiing operations concerns at a non-towered airport.

2.   Exhibits instructional knowledge of common errors related to landplane taxiing by describing:

     a.   Improper use of brakes.
     b.   Improper positioning of the flight controls for various wind conditions.
     c.   Hazards of taxiing too fast.
     d.   Hazards associated with the failure to comply with airport/taxiway surface marking, signals, and ATC clearances or instructions.

e.　Hazards of becoming distracted while taxiing.
　　　f.　Hazards associated with failing to adhere to sterile cockpit procedures.

　3.　Demonstrates and simultaneously explains landplane taxiing from an instructional standpoint.
　4.　Analyzes and corrects simulated common errors related to landplane taxiing.

Task E:　Taxiing—Seaplane (ASES)

References:　FAA-H-8083-3, FAA-H-8083-23, FAA-S-8081-12, FAA-S-ACS-6; POH/AFM; USCG Navigation Rules, International-Inland.

Objective:　To determine that the applicant:

　1.　Exhibits instructional knowledge of the elements of seaplane taxiing by describing:

　　　a.　Wind effect.
　　　b.　Prevention of porpoising and skipping.
　　　c.　Selection of the most suitable course for taxiing, following available marking aids.
　　　d.　Conditions in which idle, plowing, and step taxiing are used.
　　　e.　Procedures for idle, plowing, and step taxiing.
　　　f.　Control positioning for various wind conditions.
　　　g.　Use of water rudders.
　　　h.　Procedures used to avoid other aircraft and hazards.
　　　i.　Procedures used to avoid excessive water spray into the propeller.
　　　j.　180° and 360° turns in idle, plowing, and step positions.
　　　k.　Application of right-of-way rules.

　2.　Exhibits instructional knowledge of common errors related to seaplane taxiing by describing:

　　　a.　Improper positioning of flight controls for various wind conditions.
　　　b.　Improper control of speed and direction.
　　　c.　Failure to prevent porpoising and skipping.
　　　d.　Failure to use the most suitable course and available marking aids.
　　　e.　Failure to use proper clearing procedures to avoid hazards.
　　　f.　Failure to apply right-of-way rules.

3. Demonstrates and simultaneously explains seaplane taxiing from an instructional standpoint.
4. Analyzes and corrects simulated common errors related to seaplane taxiing.

Task F: Sailing (ASES)

References: FAA-H-8083-3, FAA-H-8083-23, FAA-S-8081-12, FAA-S-ACS-6; POH/AFM, USCG Navigation Rules, International-Inland.

Objective: To determine that the applicant:

1. Exhibits instructional knowledge of the elements of sailing by describing:

   a. Procedures used in sailing (engine idling or shut down, as appropriate).
   b. Conditions and situations where sailing would be used.
   c. Selection of the most favorable course to follow.
   d. Use of flight controls, flaps, doors, and water rudders to follow the selected course.
   e. Procedures used to change direction from downwind to crosswind.
   f. Control of speed.

2. Exhibits instructional knowledge of common errors related to sailing by describing:

   a. Failure to select the most favorable course to destination.
   b. Improper use of controls, flaps, and water rudders.
   c. Improper procedure when changing direction.
   d. Improper procedure for speed control.

3. Demonstrates and simultaneously explains sailing from an instructional standpoint.
4. Analyzes and corrects simulated common errors related to sailing.

Task G: Before Takeoff Check (ASEL and ASES)

References: FAA-H-8083-3, FAA-H-8083-23, FAA-S-8081-12, FAA-S-ACS-6; POH/AFM.

Objective: To determine that the applicant:

1. Exhibits instructional knowledge of the elements of the before takeoff check by describing:

a. Positioning the airplane with consideration for other aircraft, surface conditions, and wind.
b. Division of attention inside and outside the cockpit.
c. Importance of following the checklist and responding to each checklist item.
d. Reasons for assuring suitable engine temperatures and pressures for run-up and takeoff.
e. Method used to determine that airplane is in a safe operating condition.
f. Importance of reviewing takeoff performance airspeeds, expected takeoff distances, and emergency procedures.
g. Method used for assuring that the takeoff area or path is free of hazards.
h. Method of avoiding runway incursions and ensuring no conflict with traffic prior to taxiing into takeoff position.

2. Exhibits instructional knowledge of common errors related to the before takeoff check by describing:

a. Failure to properly use the appropriate checklist.
b. Improper positioning of the airplane.
c. Improper acceptance of marginal engine performance.
d. An improper check of flight controls.
e. Hazards of failure to review takeoff and emergency procedures.
f. Failure to avoid runway incursions and to ensure no conflict with traffic prior to taxiing into takeoff position.

3. Demonstrates and simultaneously explains a before takeoff check from an instructional standpoint.
4. Analyzes and corrects simulated common errors related to a before takeoff check.

VI. Airport and Seaplane Base Operations

Note: *The examiner must select at least one Task.*

Task A: *Radio Communications and ATC Light Signals (ASEL and ASES)*

References: *AIM; FAA-H-8083-3, FAA-H-8083-25, FAA-S-8081-12, FAA-S-ACS-6.*

Objective: To determine that the applicant:

1. Exhibits instructional knowledge of the elements of radio communications and ATC light signals by describing:

    a. Selection and use of appropriate radio frequencies.
    b. Recommended procedure and phraseology for radio communications.
    c. Receipt of, acknowledgement of, and compliance with ATC clearances and instructions.
    d. Interpretation of and compliance with ATC light signals.

2. Exhibits instructional knowledge of common errors related to radio communications and ATC light signals by describing:

    a. Use of improper frequencies.
    b. improper procedure and phraseology when using radio communications, such as neglecting to state the aircraft call sign/n number at non-towered airports, failure to state position, runway of takeoff, and the airport of operation.
    c. Failure to acknowledge, or properly comply with, ATC clearances and instructions.
    d. Failure to understand, or to properly comply with, ATC light signals.

3. Demonstrates and simultaneously explains radio communication procedures from an instructional standpoint.
4. Analyzes and corrects simulated common errors related to radio communications and ATC light signals.

Task B: *Traffic Patterns (ASEL and ASES)*

References: *AC 90-42, AC 90-66, AIM; FAA-H-8083-3, FAA-H-8083-25, FAA-S-8081-12, FAA-S-ACS-6.*

Objective: To determine that the applicant:

1. Exhibits instructional knowledge of the elements of traffic patterns by describing:

   a. Operations at airports and seaplane bases with and without operating control towers.
   b. Adherence to traffic pattern procedures, instructions, and rules.
   c. How to maintain proper spacing from other traffic.
   d. How to maintain the desired ground track.
   e. Wind shear and wake turbulence avoidance procedures.
   f. Orientation with the runway or landing area in use.
   g. How to establish a final approach at an appropriate distance from the runway or landing area.
   h. Use of checklist.

2. Exhibits instructional knowledge of common errors related to traffic patterns by describing:

   a. Failure to comply with traffic pattern instructions, procedures, and rules.
   b. Improper correction for wind drift.
   c. Inadequate spacing from other traffic.
   d. Poor altitude or airspeed control.

3. Demonstrates and simultaneously explains traffic patterns from an instructional standpoint.
4. Analyzes and corrects simulated common errors related to traffic patterns.

Task C: Airport/Seaplane Base, Runway and Taxiway Signs, Markings, and Lighting (ASEL and ASES)

References: AIM; AC 91-73, AC 150/5340-1, AC 150/5340-18; FAA-H-8083-23, FAA-H-8083-25, FAA-S-8081-12, FAA-S-ACS-6.

Objective: To determine that the applicant:

1. Exhibits instructional knowledge of the elements of airport/ seaplane base runway and taxiway signs, markings, and lighting by describing:

   a. Identification and proper interpretation of airport/seaplane base, runway and taxiway signs and markings with emphasis on runway incursion avoidance.
   b. Identification and proper interpretation of airport/seaplane base, runway and taxiway lighting with emphasis on runway incursion avoidance.

2. Exhibits instructional knowledge of common errors related to airport/seaplane base, runway and taxiway signs, markings, and lighting by describing:

   a. Failure to comply with airport/seaplane base, runway and taxiway signs and markings.
   b. Failure to comply with airport/seaplane base, runway and taxiway lighting.
   c. Failure to use proper runway incursion avoidance procedures.

3. Demonstrates and simultaneously explains airport/seaplane base, runway and taxiway signs, markings, and lighting from an instructional standpoint.
4. Analyzes and corrects simulated common errors related to airport/seaplane base, runway and taxiway signs, markings, and lighting.

VII. Takeoffs, Landings, and Go-Arounds

Note: The examiner must select at least two takeoff and two landing Tasks.

Task A: Normal and Crosswind Takeoff and Climb (ASEL and ASES)

References: FAA-H-8083-3, FAA-H-8083-23, FAA-S-8081-12, FAA-S-ACS-6; POH/AFM.

Objective: To determine that the applicant:

1. Exhibits instructional knowledge of the elements of a normal and crosswind takeoff and climb by describing:

   a. Procedures before taxiing onto the runway or takeoff area to ensure runway incursion avoidance. Verify ATC clearance/no aircraft on final at non-towered airports before entering the runway, and ensure correct takeoff runway positioning of the airplane with consideration for other aircraft, surface conditions, and wind.
   b. Normal and crosswind takeoff and lift-off procedures.
   c. Difference between a normal and a glassy-water takeoff (ASES).
   d. Proper climb attitude, power setting, and airspeed (V_Y).
   e. Proper use of checklist.

2. Exhibits instructional knowledge of common errors related to a normal and crosswind takeoff and climb by describing:

   a. Improper runway incursion avoidance procedures.
   b. Improper use of controls during a normal or crosswind takeoff.
   c. Inappropriate lift-off procedures.
   d. Improper climb attitude, power setting, and airspeed (V_Y).
   e. Improper use of checklist.

3. Demonstrates and simultaneously explains a normal or a crosswind takeoff and climb from an instructional standpoint.
4. Analyzes and corrects simulated common errors related to a normal or a crosswind takeoff and climb.

**Task B: Short-Field (Confined Area ASES) Takeoff and
Maximum Performance Climb (ASEL and ASES)**

References: *FAA-H-8083-3, FAA-H-8083-2, FAA-S-8081-12,
FAA-S-ACS-6; POH/AFM.*

Objective: To determine that the applicant:

1. Exhibits instructional knowledge of the elements of a short-field takeoff and climb by describing:

    a. Procedures before taxiing onto the runway or takeoff area to ensure runway incursion avoidance. Verify ATC clearance/no aircraft on final at non-towered airports before entering the runway, and ensure correct takeoff runway positioning of the airplane with consideration for other aircraft, surface conditions, and wind.
    b. Short-field takeoff and lift-off procedures.
    c. Initial climb attitude and airspeed (V_x) until obstacle is cleared (50 feet AGL).
    d. Proper use of checklist.

2. Exhibits instructional knowledge of common errors related to a short-field takeoff and climb by describing:

    a. Improper runway incursion avoidance procedures.
    b. Improper use of controls during a short-field takeoff.
    c. Improper lift-off procedures.
    d. Improper initial climb attitude, power setting, and airspeed (V_x) to clear obstacle.
    e. Improper use of checklist.

3. Demonstrates and simultaneously explains a short-field takeoff and climb from an instructional standpoint.
4. Analyzes and corrects simulated common errors related to a short-field takeoff and climb.

Task C: Soft-Field Takeoff and Climb (ASEL)

References: *FAA-H-8083-3, FAA-S-8081-12, FAA-S-ACS-6;
POH/AFM.*

Objective: To determine that the applicant:

1. Exhibits instructional knowledge of the elements of a soft-field takeoff and climb by describing:

    a. Procedures before taxiing onto the runway or takeoff area to ensure runway incursion avoidance. Verify ATC clearance/no aircraft on final at non-towered airports before entering the runway, and ensure that correct takeoff runway positioning of the airplane with consideration for other aircraft, surface conditions, and wind.

    b.   Soft-field takeoff and lift-off procedures.

    c.   Initial climb attitude and airspeed, (V_X, if an obstacle is present (50 feet AGL), or V_Y).

    d.   Proper use of checklist.

2.   Exhibits instructional knowledge of common errors related to a soft-field takeoff and climb by describing:

    a.   Improper runway incursion avoidance procedures.

    b.   Improper use of controls during a soft-field takeoff.

    c.   Improper lift-off procedures.

    d.   Improper climb attitude, power setting, and airspeed (V_Y or V_X).

    e.   Improper use of checklist.

3.   Demonstrates and simultaneously explains a soft-field takeoff and climb from an instructional standpoint.

4.   Analyzes and corrects simulated common errors related to a soft-field takeoff and climb.

Task D: *Glassy-Water Takeoff and Climb (ASES)*

References: *AC 91-69; FAA-H-8083-3, FAA-H-8083-23, FAA-S-8081-12, FAA-S-ACS-6; POH/AFM.*

Objective: To determine that the applicant:

1.   Exhibits instructional knowledge of the elements of a glassy-water takeoff and climb by describing:

    a.   Procedures before taxiing onto the takeoff area to ensure waterway is clear of objects or obstructions.

    b.   Flight control, flap, and water rudder use during glassy-water takeoff procedures.

    c.   Appropriate planning attitude and lift-off procedures on glassy water.

    d.   Initial climb attitude and airspeed (V_X, if an obstacle is present (50 feet AGL), or V_Y).

    e.   Proper use of after takeoff checklist.

2.   Exhibits instructional knowledge of common errors related to a glassy-water takeoff and climb by describing:

    a.   Improper takeoff water way clearance procedures.

    b.   Poor judgment in the selection of a suitable takeoff area.

    c.   Improper use of controls during a glassy-water takeoff.

    d.   Inappropriate lift-off procedures.

     e. Hazards of inadvertent contact with the water after becoming airborne.

     f. Improper climb attitude, power setting, and airspeed (V_Y or V_X).

     g. Improper use of checklist.

3. Demonstrates and simultaneously explains a glassy-water takeoff and climb from an instructional standpoint.

4. Analyzes and corrects simulated common errors related to a glassy-water takeoff and climb.

Task E: Rough-Water Takeoff and Climb (ASES)

References: FAA-H-8083-3, FAA-H-8083-23, FAA-S-8081-12, FAA-S-ACS-6; POH/AFM.

Objective: To determine that the applicant:

1. Exhibits instructional knowledge of the elements of a rough-water takeoff and climb by describing:

     a. Procedures before taxiing onto the takeoff area to ensure waterway is clear of objects or obstructions.

     b. Flight control, flap and water rudder use during rough-water takeoff procedures.

     c. Appropriate planning attitude and lift-off procedures on rough water.

     d. Initial climb attitude and airspeed (V_X, if an obstacle is present (50 feet AGL), or V_Y).

     e. Proper use of after takeoff checklist.

2. Exhibits instructional knowledge of common errors related to a rough-water takeoff and climb by describing:

     a. Improper takeoff water way clearance procedures.

     b. Poor judgment in the selection of a suitable takeoff area.

     c. Improper use of controls during a rough-water takeoff.

     d. Inappropriate lift-off procedures.

     e. Hazards of inadvertent contact with the water after becoming airborne.

     f. Improper climb attitude, power setting, and airspeed (V_Y or V_X).

     g. Improper use of checklist.

3. Demonstrates and simultaneously explains a rough-water takeoff and climb from an instructional standpoint.

4. Analyzes and corrects simulated common errors related to a rough-water takeoff and climb.

Task F: Normal and Crosswind Approach and Landing (ASEL and ASES)

References: AC 91-73; FAA-H-8083-3, FAA-H-8083-23, FAA-S-8081-12, FAA-S-ACS-6; POH/AFM.

Objective: To determine that the applicant:

1. Exhibits instructional knowledge of the elements of a normal and a crosswind approach and landing by describing:

   a. How to determine landing performance and limitations.
   b. Configuration, power, and trim.
   c. Obstructions and other hazards which should be considered.
   d. A stabilized approach at the recommended airspeed to the selected touchdown area.
   e. Course of action if selected touchdown area is going to be missed.
   f. Coordination of flight controls.
   g. A precise ground track.
   h. Wind shear and wake turbulence avoidance procedures.
   i. Most suitable crosswind procedure.
   j. Timing, judgment, and control procedure during roundout and touchdown.
   k. Directional control after touchdown.
   l. Use of brakes (landplane).
   m. Use of checklist.
   n. After landing runway incursion avoidance procedures.

2. Exhibits instructional knowledge of common errors related to a normal and a crosswind approach and landing by describing:

   a. Improper use of landing performance data and limitations.
   b. Failure to establish approach and landing configuration at appropriate time or in proper sequence.
   c. Failure to establish and maintain a stabilized approach.
   d. Inappropriate removal of hand from throttle.
   e. Improper procedure during roundout and touchdown.
   f. Poor directional control after touchdown.
   g. Improper use of brakes (ASEL).
   h. Failure to ensure receipt and acknowledgement of landing clearance.
   i. Failure to review airport diagram for runway exit situational awareness to avoid a runway incursion after landing.

3. Demonstrates and simultaneously explains a normal or a crosswind approach and landing from an instructional standpoint.
4. Analyzes and corrects simulated common errors related to a normal or crosswind approach and landing.

Task G: Slip to a Landing (ASEL and ASES)

References: FAA-H-8083-3, FAA-H-8083-23, FAA-S-ACS-6; POH/AFM.

Objective: To determine that the applicant:

1. Exhibits instructional knowledge of the elements of a slip (forward and side) to a landing by describing:

   a. Configuration, power, and trim.
   b. Obstructions and other hazards which should be considered.
   c. A stabilized slip at the appropriate airspeed to the selected touchdown area.
   d. Possible airspeed indication errors.
   e. Proper application of flight controls.
   f. A precise ground track.
   g. Wind shear and wake turbulence avoidance procedures.
   h. Timing, judgment, and control procedure during transition from slip to touchdown.
   i. Directional control after touchdown.
   j. Use of brakes (ASEL).
   k. Use of checklist.
   l. After landing runway incursion avoidance procedures.

2. Exhibits instructional knowledge of common errors related to a slip (forward and side) to a landing by describing:

   a. Improper use of landing performance data and limitations.
   b. Failure to establish approach and landing configuration at appropriate time or in proper sequence.
   c. Failure to maintain a stabilized slip.
   d. Inappropriate removal of hand from throttle.
   e. Improper procedure during transition from the slip to the touchdown.
   f. Poor directional control after touchdown.
   g. Improper use of brakes (landplane).

3. Demonstrates and simultaneously explains a forward or sideslip to a landing from an instructional standpoint.

4. Analyzes and corrects simulated common errors related to a forward or sideslip to a landing.

Task H: Go-Around/Rejected Landing (ASEL and ASES)

References: FAA-H-8083-3, FAA-H-8083-23, FAA-S-8081-12, FAA-S-ACS-6; POH/AFM.

Objective: To determine that the applicant:

1. Exhibits instructional knowledge of the elements of a go-around/rejected landing by describing:

    a. Situations where a go-around/rejected landing is necessary.
    b. Importance of making a prompt decision.
    c. Importance of applying takeoff power immediately after the go-around/rejected landing decision is made.
    d. Importance of establishing proper pitch attitude.
    e. Wing flaps retraction, if applicable.
    f. Use of trim.
    g. Landing gear retraction, if applicable.
    h. Proper climb speed.
    i. Proper track and obstruction clearance.
    j. Use of checklist.

2. Exhibits instructional knowledge of common errors related to a go-around/rejected landing by describing:

    a. Failure to recognize a situation where a go-around/rejected landing is necessary.
    b. Hazards of delaying a decision to go-around/rejected landing.
    c. Improper power application.
    d. Failure to control pitch attitude.
    e. Failure to compensate for torque effect.
    f. Improper trim procedure.
    g. Failure to maintain recommended airspeeds.
    h. Improper wing flaps or landing gear retraction procedure, if applicable.
    i. Failure to maintain proper track during climb-out.
    j. Failure to remain well clear of obstructions and other traffic.

3. Demonstrates and simultaneously explains a go-around/rejected landing from an instructional standpoint.
4. Analyzes and corrects simulated common errors related to a go-around/rejected landing.

Task I: *Short-Field (Confined Area (ASES)) Approach and Landing (ASEL and ASES)*

References: FAA-H-8083-3, FAA-H-8083-23, FAA-S-8081-12, FAA-S-ACS-6; POH/AFM.

Objective: To determine that the applicant:

1. Exhibits instructional knowledge of the elements of a short-field approach and landing by describing:

   a. How to determine landing performance and limitations.
   b. Configuration and trim.
   c. Proper use of pitch and power to maintain desired approach angle.
   d. Obstructions and other hazards which should be considered.
   e. Effect of wind.
   f. Selection of touchdown and go-around points.
   g. A stabilized approach at the recommended airspeed to the selected touchdown point.
   h. Coordination of flight controls.
   i. A precise ground track.
   j. Timing, judgment, and control procedure during roundout and touchdown.
   k. Directional control after touchdown.
   l. Use of brakes (ASEL).
   m. Use of checklist.
   n. After-landing runway incursion avoidance procedures.

2. Exhibits instructional knowledge of common errors related to a short-field approach and landing by describing:

   a. Improper use of landing performance data and limitations.
   b. Failure to establish approach and landing configuration at appropriate time or in proper sequence.
   c. Failure to establish and maintain a stabilized approach.
   d. Improper procedure in use of power, wing flaps, and trim.
   e. Inappropriate removal of hand from throttle.
   f. Improper procedure during roundout and touchdown.
   g. Poor directional control after touchdown.
   h. Improper use of brakes.

3. Demonstrates and simultaneously explains a short-field approach and landing from an instructional standpoint.
4. Analyzes and corrects simulated common errors related to a short-field approach and landing.

Task J: Soft-Field Approach and Landing (ASEL)

References: FAA-H-8083-3, FAA-S-8081-12, FAA-S-ACS-6; POH/AFM.

Objective: To determine that the applicant:

1. Exhibits instructional knowledge of the elements of a soft-field approach and landing by describing:

   a. How to determine landing performance and limitations.
   b. Configuration and trim.
   c. Obstructions and other hazards which should be considered.
   d. Effect of wind and landing surface.
   e. Selection of a touchdown area.
   f. A stabilized approach at the recommended airspeed to the selected touchdown point.
   g. Coordination of flight controls.
   h. A precise ground track.
   i. Timing, judgment, and control procedure during roundout and touchdown.
   j. Touchdown in a nose-high pitch attitude at minimum safe airspeed.
   k. Proper use of power.
   l. Directional control after touchdown.
   m. Use of checklist.
   n. After landing runway incursion avoidance procedures.

2. Exhibits instructional knowledge of common errors related to a soft-field approach and landing by describing:

   a. Improper use of landing performance data and limitations.
   b. Failure to establish approach and landing configuration at appropriate time or in proper sequence.
   c. Failure to establish and maintain a stabilized approach.
   d. Failure to consider the effect of wind and landing surface.
   e. Improper procedure in use of power, wing flaps, and trim.
   f. Inappropriate removal of hand from throttle.
   g. Improper procedure during roundout and touchdown.
   h. Failure to hold back elevator pressure after touchdown.
   i. Closing the throttle too soon after touchdown.
   j. Poor directional control after touchdown.
   k. Improper use of brakes.

3. Demonstrates and simultaneously explains a soft-field approach and landing from an instructional standpoint.

4. Analyzes and corrects simulated common errors related to a soft-field approach and landing.

Task K: Power-Off 180° Accuracy Approach and Landing (ASEL)

References: FAA-H-8083-3, FAA-S-8081-12.

Objective: To determine that the applicant:

1. Exhibits instructional knowledge of the elements of a 180° power-off accuracy approach and landing by describing:

   a. Configuration and trim.
   b. Effects of wind and selection of a touchdown area.
   c. The key points in the pattern.
   d. A stabilized approach at the recommended airspeed to the selected touchdown area.
   e. Coordination of flight controls.
   f. Timing, judgment, and control procedure during roundout and touchdown.
   g. Directional control after touchdown.
   h. Use of checklist.
   i. After landing runway incursion avoidance procedures.

2. Exhibits instructional knowledge of common errors related to a 180° power-off accuracy approach and landing by describing:

   a. Failure to establish approach and landing configuration at proper time or in proper sequence.
   b. Failure to identify the key points in the pattern.
   c. Failure to establish and maintain a stabilized approach.
   d. Failure to consider the effect of wind and landing surface.
   e. Improper use of power, wing flaps, or trim.
   f. Improper procedure during roundout and touchdown.
   g. Failure to hold back elevator pressure after touchdown.
   h. Poor directional control after touchdown.
   i. Improper use of brakes.

3. Demonstrates and simultaneously explains a 180° power-off accuracy approach and landing from an instructional standpoint.
4. Analyzes and corrects simulated common errors related to a 180° power-off accuracy approach and landing.

Task L: Glassy-Water Approach and Landing (ASES)

References: *FAA-H-8083-3, FAA-H-8083-23, FAA-S-8081-12, FAA-S-ACS-6; POH/AFM.*

Objective: To determine that the applicant:

1. Exhibits instructional knowledge of the elements of a glassy-water approach and landing by describing:

    a. How to determine landing performance and limitations.
    b. Configuration and trim.
    c. Deceptive characteristics of glassy water.
    d. Selection of a suitable landing area and go-around point.
    e. Terrain and obstructions which should be considered.
    f. Detection of hazards in the landing area such as shallow water, obstructions, or floating debris.
    g. Coordination of flight controls.
    h. A precise ground track.
    i. A power setting and pitch attitude that will result in the recommended airspeed and rate of descent throughout the final approach to touchdown.
    j. How to maintain positive control after landing.
    k. Use of checklist.

2. Exhibits instructional knowledge of common errors related to a glassy-water approach and landing by describing:

    a. Improper use of landing performance data and limitations.
    b. Failure to establish approach and landing configuration at the appropriate time and in proper sequence.
    c. Failure to establish and maintain a stabilized approach at the recommended airspeed and rate of descent.
    d. Improper procedure in use of power, wing flaps, or trim.
    e. Inappropriate removal of hand from throttle.
    f. Failure to touch down with power in the proper stabilized attitude.
    g. Failure to maintain positive control after landing.

3. Demonstrates and simultaneously explains a glassy-water approach and landing from an instructional standpoint.
4. Analyzes and corrects simulated common errors related to a glassy-water approach and landing.

FAA-S-8081-6D

Task M: Rough-Water Approach and Landing (ASES)

References: *FAA-H-8083-3, FAA-H-8083-23, FAA-S-8081-12, FAA-S-ACS-6; POH/AFM.*

Objective: To determine that the applicant:

1.   Exhibits instructional knowledge of the elements of a rough-water approach and landing by describing:

   a.   How to determine landing performance and limitations.
   b.   Review of wind conditions.
   c.   How landing area characteristics can be evaluated.
   d.   Selection of a suitable landing area and go-around point.
   e.   Terrain and obstructions which should be considered.
   f.   Detection of hazards in the landing area such as shallow water, obstructions, or floating debris.
   g.   Configuration and trim.
   h.   Coordination of flight controls.
   i.   A precise ground track.
   j.   A stabilized approach at the recommended airspeed to the selected touchdown area.
   k.   Timing, judgment, and control procedure during roundout and touchdown.
   l.   Maintenance of positive control after landing.
   m.   Use of checklist.

2.   Exhibits instructional knowledge of common errors related to a rough-water approach and landing by describing:

   a.   Improper use of landing performance data and limitations.
   b.   Failure to establish approach and landing configuration at appropriate time or in proper sequence.
   c.   Failure to establish and maintain a stabilized approach.
   d.   Improper procedure in use of power, wing flaps, or trim.
   e.   Inappropriate removal of hand from throttle.
   f.   Improper procedure during roundout and touchdown.
   g.   Failure to maintain positive control after landing.

3.   Demonstrates and simultaneously explains a rough-water approach and landing from an instructional standpoint.
4.   Analyzes and corrects simulated common errors related a rough-water approach and landing.

VIII. Fundamentals of Flight

Note: *The examiner must select at least one Task.*

Task A: *Straight-and-Level Flight (ASEL and ASES)*

References: FAA-H-8083-3, FAA-H-8083-23, FAA-S-ACS-6.

Objective: To determine that the applicant:

1. Exhibits instructional knowledge of the elements of straight-and-level flight by describing:

   a. Effect and use of flight controls.
   b. The integrated flight instruction method.
   c. Outside and instrument references used for pitch, bank, yaw, and power control; the cross-check and interpretation of those references; and the control procedure used.
   d. Trim procedure.
   e. Methods that can be used to overcome tenseness and overcontrolling.

2. Exhibits instructional knowledge of common errors related to straight-and-level flight by describing:

   a. Failure to cross-check and correctly interpret outside and instrument references.
   b. Application of control movements rather than pressures.
   c. Uncoordinated use of flight controls.
   d. Faulty trim procedure.

3. Demonstrates and simultaneously explains straight-and-level flight from an instructional standpoint.
4. Analyzes and corrects simulated common errors related to straight-and-level flight.

Task B: *Level Turns (ASEL and ASES)*

References: FAA-H-8083-3, FAA-S-ACS-6.

Objective: To determine that the applicant:

1. Exhibits instructional knowledge of the elements of level turns by describing:

   a. Effect and use of flight controls.
   b. The Integrated Flight Instruction method.
   c. Outside and instrument references used for pitch, bank, yaw, and power control; the cross-check and

interpretation of those references; and the control procedure used.

    d.   Trim procedure.

    e.   Methods that can be used to overcome tenseness and overcontrolling.

2.   Exhibits instructional knowledge of common errors related to level turns by describing:

    a.   Failure to cross-check and correctly interpret outside and instrument references.

    b.   Application of control movements rather than pressures.

    c.   Uncoordinated use of flight controls.

    d.   Faulty altitude and bank control.

3.   Demonstrates and simultaneously explains level turns from an instructional standpoint.

4.   Analyzes and corrects simulated common errors related to level turns.

Task C: Straight Climbs and Climbing Turns (ASEL AND ASES)

References: FAA-H-8083-3, FAA-S-ACS-6.

Objective: To determine that the applicant:

1.   Exhibits instructional knowledge of the elements of straight climbs and climbing turns by describing:

    a.   Effect and use of flight controls.

    b.   The Integrated Flight Instruction method.

    c.   Outside and instrument references used for pitch, bank, yaw, and power control; the cross-check and interpretation of those references; and the control procedure used.

    d.   Trim procedure.

    e.   Methods that can be used to overcome tenseness and overcontrolling.

2.   Exhibits instructional knowledge of common errors related to straight climbs and climbing turns by describing:

    a.   Failure to cross-check and correctly interpret outside and instrument references.

    b.   Application of control movements rather than pressures.

    c.   Improper correction for torque effect.

    d.   Faulty trim procedure.

3. Demonstrates and simultaneously explains straight climbs and climbing turns from an instructional standpoint.
4. Analyzes and corrects simulated common errors related to straight climbs and climbing turns.

Task D: Straight Descents and Descending Turns (ASEL and ASES)

References: FAA-H-8083-3, FAA-S-ACS-6.

Objective: To determine that the applicant:

1. Exhibits instructional knowledge of the elements of straight descents and descending turns by describing:

    a. Effect and use of flight controls.
    b. The Integrated Flight Instruction method.
    c. Outside and instrument references used for pitch, bank, yaw, and power control; the cross-check and interpretation of those references; and the control procedure used.
    d. Trim procedure.
    e. Methods that can be used to overcome tenseness and overcontrolling.

2. Exhibits instructional knowledge of common errors related to straight descents and descending turns by describing:

    a. Failure to cross-check and correctly interpret outside and instrument references.
    b. Application of control movements rather than pressures.
    c. Uncoordinated use of flight controls.
    d. Faulty trim procedure.
    e. Failure to clear engine and to use carburetor heat, as appropriate.

3. Demonstrates and simultaneously explains straight descents and descending turns from an instructional standpoint.
4. Analyzes and corrects simulated common errors related to straight descents and descending turns.

IX. Performance Maneuvers

Note: *The examiner must select at least Tasks A or B and C or D.*

Task A: *Steep Turns (ASEL and ASES)*

References: FAA-H-8083-3, FAA-S-8081-12, FAA-S-ACS-6; POH/AFM.

Objective: To determine that the applicant:

1. Exhibits instructional knowledge of the elements of steep turns by describing:

   a. Relationship of bank angle, load factor, and stalling speed.
   b. Overbanking tendency.
   c. Torque effect in right and left turns.
   d. Selection of a suitable altitude.
   e. Orientation, division of attention, and planning.
   f. Entry and rollout procedure.
   g. Coordination of flight and power controls.
   h. Altitude, bank, and power control during the turn.
   i. Proper recovery to straight-and-level flight.

2. Exhibits instructional knowledge of common errors related to steep turns by describing:

   a. Improper pitch, bank, and power coordination during entry and rollout.
   b. Uncoordinated use of flight controls.
   c. Improper procedure in correcting altitude deviations.
   d. Loss of orientation.

3. Demonstrates and simultaneously explains steep turns from an instructional standpoint.
4. Analyzes and corrects simulated common errors related to steep turns.

Task B: *Steep Spirals (ASEL and ASES)*

References: FAA-H-8083-3, FAA-S-8081-12.

Objective: To determine that the applicant:

1. Exhibits instructional knowledge of the elements of steep spirals by describing:

   a. The purpose of steep spirals and their relationship to emergency landing procedures.
   b. Selection of entry altitude.

    c. Entry airspeed and power setting.
    d. Selection of a proper ground reference point.
    e. Division of attention and planning.
    f. Coordination of flight controls.
    g. Maintenance of constant radius around selected point.
    h. Maintenance of constant airspeed throughout maneuver.

2. Exhibits instructional knowledge of common errors related to steep spiral by describing:

    a. Improper pitch, bank, yaw, and power coordination during entry or completion.
    b. Uncoordinated use of flight controls.
    c. Improper planning and lack of maintenance of constant airspeed and radius.
    d. Failure to stay orientated to the number of turns and the rollout heading.

3. Demonstrates and simultaneously explains a steep spiral from an instructional standpoint.
4. Analyzes and corrects simulated common errors related to steep spirals.

Task C: Chandelles (ASEL and ASES)

References: FAA-H-8083-3; FAA-S-8081-12.

Objective: To determine that the applicant:

1. Exhibits instructional knowledge of the elements of chandelles by describing:

    a. The purpose of chandelles and their relationship to basic/advanced airmanship skills.
    b. Selection of entry altitude.
    c. Entry airspeed and power setting.
    d. Division of attention and planning.
    e. Coordination of flight controls.
    f. Pitch and bank attitudes at various points during the maneuver.
    g. Proper correction for torque effect in right and left turns.
    h. Achievement of maximum performance.
    i. Completion procedure.

2. Exhibits instructional knowledge of common errors related to chandelles by describing:

    a. Improper pitch, bank, and power coordination during entry or completion.

b. Uncoordinated use of flight controls.
c. Improper planning and timing of pitch and bank attitude changes.
d. Factors related to failure in achieving maximum performance.
e. A stall during the maneuver.

3. Demonstrates and simultaneously explains chandelles from an instructional standpoint.
4. Analyzes and corrects simulated common errors related to chandelles.

Task D: Lazy Eights (ASEL and ASES)

References: FAA-H-8083-3, FAA-S-8081-12.

Objective: To determine that the applicant:

1. Exhibits instructional knowledge of the elements of lazy eights by describing:

   a. The purpose of lazy eights and their relationship to basic/advanced airmanship skills.
   b. Selection of entry altitude.
   c. Selection of suitable reference points.
   d. Entry airspeed and power setting.
   e. Entry procedure.
   f. Orientation, division of attention, and planning.
   g. Coordination of flight controls.
   h. Pitch and bank attitudes at key points during the maneuver.
   i. Importance of consistent airspeed and altitude control at key points during the maneuver.
   j. Proper correction for torque effect in right and left turns.
   k. Loop symmetry.

2. Exhibits instructional knowledge of common errors related to lazy eights by describing:

   a. Poor selection of reference points.
   b. Uncoordinated use of flight controls.
   c. Unsymmetrical loops resulting from poorly planned pitch and bank attitude changes.
   d. Inconsistent airspeed and altitude at key points.
   e. Loss of orientation.
   f. Excessive deviation from reference points.

3. Demonstrates and simultaneously explains lazy eights from an instructional standpoint.

4.   Analyzes and corrects simulated common errors related to lazy eights.

X.   Ground Reference Maneuvers

Note: *The examiner must select Task D and one other Task.*

Task A: *Rectangular Course (ASEL and ASES)*

References: FAA-H-8083-3, FAA-S-ACS-6.

Objective: To determine that the applicant:

1.   Exhibits instructional knowledge of the elements of a rectangular course by describing:

   a.   How to select a suitable altitude.
   b.   How to select a suitable ground reference with consideration given to emergency landing areas.
   c.   Orientation, division of attention, and planning.
   d.   Configuration and airspeed prior to entry.
   e.   Relationship of a rectangular course to an airport traffic pattern.
   f.   Wind drifts correction.
   g.   How to maintain desired altitude, airspeed, and distance from ground reference boundaries.
   h.   Timing of turn entries and rollouts.
   i.   Coordination of flight controls.

2.   Exhibits instructional knowledge of common errors related to a rectangular course by describing:

   a.   Poor planning, orientation, or division of attention.
   b.   Uncoordinated use of flight controls.
   c.   Improper correction for wind drift.
   d.   Failure to maintain selected altitude or airspeed.
   e.   Selection of a ground reference where there is no suitable emergency landing area within gliding distance.

3.   Demonstrates and simultaneously explains a rectangular course from an instructional standpoint.
4.   Analyzes and corrects simulated common errors related to a rectangular course.

Task B: *S-Turns across a Road (ASEL and ASES)*

References: FAA-H-8083-3, FAA-S-ACS-6.

Objective: To determine that the applicant:

1.   Exhibits instructional knowledge of the elements of S-turns across a road by describing:

    a.   The purpose of S-turns across a road and their relationship to basic/advanced airmanship skills.
    b.   How to select a suitable altitude.
    c.   How to select a suitable ground reference line with consideration given to emergency landing areas.
    d.   Orientation, division of attention, and planning.
    e.   Configuration and airspeed prior to entry.
    f.   Entry procedure.
    g.   Wind drifts correction.
    h.   Tracking of semicircles of equal radii on either side of the selected ground reference line.
    i.   How to maintain desired altitude and airspeed.
    j.   Turn reversal over the ground reference line.
    k.   Coordination of flight controls.

2.   Exhibits instructional knowledge of common errors related to S-turns across a road by describing:

    a.   Faulty entry procedure.
    b.   Poor planning, orientation, or division of attention.
    c.   Uncoordinated use of flight controls.
    d.   Improper correction for wind drift.
    e.   An unsymmetrical ground track.
    f.   Failure to maintain selected altitude or airspeed.
    g.   Selection of a ground reference line where there is no suitable emergency landing area within gliding distance.

3.   Demonstrates and simultaneously explains S-turns across a road from an instructional standpoint.
4.   Analyzes and corrects simulated common errors related to S-turns across a road.

Task C: Turns Around a Point (ASEL and ASES)

References: FAA-H-8083-3; FAA-S-ACS-6.

Objective: To determine that the applicant:

1.   Exhibits instructional knowledge of the elements of turns around a point by describing:

    a.   The purpose of turns around a point and their relationship to basic/advanced airmanship skills.
    b.   How to select a suitable altitude.
    c.   How to select a suitable ground reference point with consideration given to emergency landing areas.
    d.   Orientation, division of attention, and planning.
    e.   Configuration and airspeed prior to entry.
    f.   Entry procedure.

g. Wind drifts correction.
h. How to maintain desired altitude, airspeed, and distance from reference point.
i. Coordination of flight controls.

2. Exhibits instructional knowledge of common errors related to turns around a point by describing:

a. Faulty entry procedure.
b. Poor planning, orientation, or division of attention.
c. Uncoordinated use of flight controls.
d. Improper correction for wind drift.
e. Failure to maintain selected altitude or airspeed.
f. Selection of a ground reference point where there is no suitable emergency landing area within gliding distance.

3. Demonstrates and simultaneously explains turns around a point from an instructional standpoint.
4. Analyzes and corrects simulated common errors related to turns around a point.

Task D: Eights on Pylons (ASEL and ASES)

References: FAA-H-8083-3, FAA-S-8081-12.

Objective: To determine that the applicant:

1. Exhibits instructional knowledge of the elements of eights on pylons by describing:

a. The purpose of eights on pylons and their relationship to basic/advanced airmanship skills.
b. How to determine the approximate pivotal altitude.
c. How to select suitable pylons with consideration given to emergency landing areas.
d. Orientation, division of attention, and planning.
e. Configuration and airspeed prior to entry.
f. Relationship of groundspeed change to the performance of the maneuver.
g. Pilot's "line-of-sight" reference to the pylon.
h. Entry procedure.
i. Procedure for maintaining "line-of-sight" on the pylon.
j. Proper planning for turn entries and rollouts.
k. How to correct for wind drift between pylons.
l. Coordination of flight controls.

2. Exhibits instructional knowledge of common errors related to eights on pylons by describing:

a. Faulty entry procedure.

b. Poor planning, orientation, and division of attention.
c. Uncoordinated use of flight controls.
d. Use of an improper "line-of-sight" reference.
e. Application of rudder alone to maintain "line-of-sight" on the pylon.
f. Improper planning for turn entries and rollouts.
g. Improper correction for wind drift between pylons.
h. Selection of pylons where there is no suitable emergency landing area within gliding distance.

3. Demonstrates and simultaneously explains eights on pylons from an instructional standpoint.
4. Analyzes and corrects simulated common errors related to eights on pylons.

XI. Slow Flight, Stalls, and Spins

Note: *The examiner must select at least one proficiency stall (Task B or C), at least one demonstration stall (Task D, E, F, or H), and Task G.*

Task A: *Maneuvering During Slow Flight (ASEL and ASES)*

References: FAA-H-8083-3, FAA-S-8081-12, FAA-S-ACS-6; POH/AFM.

Objective: To determine that the applicant:

1. Exhibits instructional knowledge of the elements of maneuvering during slow flight by describing:

    a. Relationship of configuration, weight, center of gravity, maneuvering loads, angle of bank, and power to flight characteristics and controllability.
    b. Relationship of the maneuver to critical flight situations, such as go-around.
    c. Performance of the maneuver with selected configurations in straight-and-level flight and level turns.
    d. Specified airspeed for the maneuver.
    e. Coordination of flight controls.
    f. Trim technique.
    g. Reestablishment of cruise flight.

2. Exhibits instructional knowledge of common errors related to maneuvering during slow flight by describing:

    a. Failure to establish specified configuration.
    b. Improper entry technique.
    c. Failure to establish and maintain the specified airspeed.
    d. Excessive variations of altitude and heading when a constant altitude and heading are specified.
    e. Uncoordinated use of flight controls.
    f. Improper correction for torque effect.
    g. Improper trim technique.
    h. Unintentional stalls.
    i. Inappropriate removal of hand from throttles.

3. Demonstrates and simultaneously explains maneuvering during slow flight from an instructional standpoint.

4. Analyzes and corrects simulated common errors related to maneuvering during slow flight.

Task B: Power-On Stalls (Proficiency) (ASEL and ASES)

References: *AC 61-67; FAA-H-8083-3, FAA-S-8081-12,*
             FAA-S-ACS-6; POH/AFM.

Objective: To determine that the applicant:

1. Exhibits instructional knowledge of the elements of power-on stalls, in climbing flight (straight or turning), with selected landing gear and flap configurations by describing:

    a. Aerodynamics of power-on stalls.
    b. Relationship of various factors such as airplane configuration, weight, center of gravity, load factor, and bank angle to stall speed.
    c. Flight situations where unintentional power-on stalls may occur.
    d. Entry technique and minimum entry altitude.
    e. Performance of power-on stalls in climbing flight (straight or turning).
    f. Coordination of flight controls.
    g. Recognition of the first indications of power-on stalls.
    h. Recovery technique and minimum recovery altitude.

2. Exhibits instructional knowledge of common errors related to power-on stalls, in climbing flight (straight or turning), with selected landing gear and flap configurations by describing:

    a. Failure to establish the specified configuration prior to entry.
    b. Improper pitch, heading, yaw, and bank control during straight-ahead stalls.
    c. Improper pitch, yaw, and bank control during turning stalls.
    d. Rough and/or uncoordinated use of flight controls.
    e. Failure to recognize the first indications of a stall.
    f. Failure to achieve a stall.
    g. Improper torque correction.
    h. Poor stall recognition and delayed recovery.
    i. Excessive altitude loss or excessive airspeed during recovery.
    j. Secondary stall during recovery.

3. Demonstrates and simultaneously explains power-on stalls, in climbing flight (straight or turning), with selected configurations, from an instructional standpoint.
4. Analyzes and corrects simulated common errors related to power-on stalls, in climbing flight (straight or turning), with selected configurations.

Task C: *Power-Off Stalls (Proficiency) (ASEL and ASES)*

References: *FAA-H-8083-3, FAA-S-8081-12, FAA-S-ACS-6; POH/AFM.*

Objective: To determine that the applicant:

1. Exhibits instructional knowledge of the elements of power-off stalls, in descending flight (straight or turning), with selected landing gear and flap configurations by describing:

    a. Aerodynamics of power-off stalls.
    b. Relationship of various factors, such as airplane configuration, weight, center of gravity, load factor, and bank angle to stall speed.
    c. Flight situations where unintentional power-off stalls may occur.
    d. Entry technique and minimum entry altitude.
    e. Performance of power-off stalls in descending flight (straight or turning).
    f. Coordination of flight controls.
    g. Recognition of the first indications of power-off stalls.
    h. Recovery technique and minimum recovery altitude.

2. Exhibits instructional knowledge of common errors related to power-off stalls, in descending flight (straight or turning), with selected landing gear and flap configurations by describing:

    a. Failure to establish the specified configuration prior to entry.
    b. Improper pitch, heading, yaw, and bank control during straight-ahead stalls.
    c. Improper pitch, yaw, and bank control during turning stalls.
    d. Rough and/or uncoordinated use of flight controls.
    e. Failure to recognize the first indications of a stall.
    f. Failure to achieve a stall.
    g. Improper torque correction.
    h. Poor stall recognition and delayed recovery.

  i. Excessive altitude loss or excessive airspeed during recovery.

  j. Secondary stall during recovery.

3. Demonstrates and simultaneously explains power-off stalls, in descending flight (straight or turning), with selected configurations, from an instructional standpoint.

4. Analyzes and corrects simulated common errors related to power-off stalls, in descending flight (straight or turning), with selected configurations.

Task D: *Cross-controlled Stalls (Demonstration) (ASEL and ASES)*

References: FAA-H-8083-3, FAA-S-8081-12, FAA-S-ACS-6; POH/AFM.

Objective: To determine that the applicant:

1. Exhibits instructional knowledge of the elements of cross-controlled stalls, with the landing gear extended by describing:

  a. Aerodynamics of cross-controlled stalls.

  b. Effects of crossed controls in gliding or reduced airspeed descending turns.

  c. Flight situations where unintentional cross-controlled stalls may occur.

  d. Entry procedure and minimum entry altitude.

  e. Recognition of cross-controlled stalls.

  f. Recovery procedure and minimum recovery altitude.

2. Exhibits instructional knowledge of common errors related to cross-controlled stalls, with the landing gear extended by describing:

  a. Failure to establish selected configuration prior to entry.

  b. Failure to establish a cross-controlled turn and stall condition that will adequately demonstrate the hazards of a cross-controlled stall.

  c. Improper or inadequate demonstration of the recognition and recovery from a cross-controlled stall.

  d. Failure to present simulated student instruction that emphasizes the hazards of a cross-controlled condition in a gliding or reduced airspeed condition.

3. Demonstrates and simultaneously explains a cross-controlled stall, with the landing gear extended, from an instructional standpoint.
4. Analyzes and corrects simulated common errors related to a cross-controlled stall with the landing gear extended.

Task E: *Elevator Trim Stalls (Demonstration) (ASEL and ASES)*

References: FAA-H-8083-3, FAA-S-8081-12, FAA-S-ACS-6; POH/AFM.

Objective: To determine that the applicant:

1. Exhibits instructional knowledge of the elements of elevator trim stalls, in selected landing gear and flap configurations by describing:

    a. Aerodynamics of elevator trims stalls.
    b. Hazards of inadequate control pressures to compensate for thrust, torque, and up-elevator trim during go-around and other related maneuvers.
    c. Entry procedure and minimum entry altitude.
    d. Recognition of elevator trims stalls.
    e. Importance of recovering from an elevator trim stall immediately upon recognition.

2. Exhibits instructional knowledge of common errors related to elevator trim stalls, in selected landing gear and flap configurations by describing:

    a. Failure to present simulated student instruction that adequately emphasizes the hazards of poor correction for torque and up-elevator trim during go-around and other maneuvers.
    b. Failure to establish selected configuration prior to entry.
    c. Improper or inadequate demonstration of the recognition of and the recovery from an elevator trim stall.

3. Demonstrates and simultaneously explains elevator trim stalls, in selected landing gear and flap configurations, from an instructional standpoint.
4. Analyzes and corrects simulated common errors related to elevator trim stalls in selected configurations.

Task F: **Secondary Stalls (Demonstration) (ASEL and ASES)**

References: *FAA-H-8083-3, FAA-S-8081-12, FAA-S-ACS-6; POH/AFM.*

Objective: To determine that the applicant:

1. Exhibits instructional knowledge of the elements of secondary stalls, in selected configurations by describing:

    a. Aerodynamics of secondary stalls.
    b. Flight situations where secondary stalls may occur.
    c. Hazards of secondary stalls during normal stall or spin recovery.
    d. Entry procedure and minimum entry altitude.
    e. Recognition of a secondary stall.
    f. Recovery procedure and minimum recovery altitude.

2. Exhibits instructional knowledge of common errors related to secondary stalls, in selected configurations by describing—

    a. Failure to establish selected configuration prior to entry.
    b. Improper or inadequate demonstration of the recognition of and recovery from a secondary stall.
    c. Failure to present simulated student instruction that adequately emphasizes the hazards of poor procedure in recovering from a primary stall.

3. Demonstrates and simultaneously explains secondary stalls, in selected landing gear and flap configurations, from an instructional standpoint.
4. Analyzes and corrects simulated common errors related to secondary stalls in selected configurations.

Task G: **Spins (ASEL)**

Note: *At the discretion of the examiner, a logbook record attesting applicant instructional competency in spin entries, spins, and spin recoveries may be accepted in lieu of this Task. The flight instructor who conducted the spin instruction must certify the logbook record.*

References: *14 CFR part 2, Type Certificate Data Sheet, AC 61-67, FAA-H-8083-3, POH/AFM.*

Objective: To determine that the applicant:

1. Exhibits instructional knowledge of the elements of spins by describing:

   a. Anxiety factors associated with spin instruction.
   b. Aerodynamics of spins.
   c. Airplanes approved for the spin maneuver based on airworthiness category and type certificate.
   d. Relationship of various factors such as configuration, weight, center of gravity, and control coordination to spins.
   e. Flight situations where unintentional spins may occur.
   f. How to recognize and recover from imminent, unintentional spins.
   g. Entry procedure and minimum entry altitude for intentional spins.
   h. Control procedure to maintain a stabilized spin.
   i. Orientation during a spin.
   j. Recovery procedure and minimum recovery altitude for intentional spins.

2. Exhibits instructional knowledge of common errors related to spins by describing:

   a. Failure to establish proper configuration prior to spin entry.
   b. Failure to achieve and maintain a full stall during spin entry.
   c. Failure to close throttle when a spin entry is achieved.
   d. Failure to recognize the indications of an imminent, unintentional spin.
   e. Improper use of flight controls during spin entry, rotation, or recovery.
   f. Disorientation during a spin.
   g. Failure to distinguish between a high-speed spiral and a spin.
   h. Excessive speed or accelerated stall during recovery.
   i. Failure to recover with minimum loss of altitude.
   j. Hazards of attempting to spin an airplane not approved for spins.

3. Demonstrates and simultaneously explains a spin (one turn) from an instructional standpoint.

4. Analyzes and corrects simulated common errors related to spins.

Task H: Accelerated Maneuver Stalls (Demonstration) (ASEL and ASES)

Note: *This Task must be completed by oral examination or demonstration at the discretion of the examiner.*

References: FAA-H-8083-3, POH/AFM.

Objective: To determine that the applicant:

1. Exhibits instructional knowledge of the elements of accelerated maneuver stalls by describing:

    a. Aerodynamics of accelerated maneuver stalls.
    b. Flight situations where accelerated maneuver stalls may occur.
    c. Hazards of accelerated stalls during stall or spin recovery.
    d. Entry procedure and minimum entry altitude.
    e. Recognition of the accelerated stall.
    f. Recovery procedure and minimum recovery altitude.

2. Demonstrates and simultaneously explains accelerated maneuver stall from an instructional standpoint.
3. Exhibits instructional knowledge of common errors related to accelerated maneuver stalls by describing:

    a. Failure to establish proper configuration prior to entry.
    b. Improper or inadequate demonstration of the recognition of and recovery from an accelerated maneuver stall.
    c. Failure to present simulated student instruction that adequately emphasizes the hazards of poor procedures in recovering from an accelerated stall.

4. Analyzes and corrects simulated common errors related to accelerated stalls.

XII. Basic Instrument Maneuvers

Note: *The examiner must select at least one Task.*

Task A: *Straight-and-Level Flight (ASEL and ASES)*

References: FAA-H-8083-3, FAA-H-8083-15, FAA-S-ACS-6.

Objective: To determine that the applicant:

1. Exhibits instructional knowledge of the elements of straight-and-level flight solely by reference to instruments by describing:

   a. Instrument cross-check, instrument interpretation, and aircraft control.
   b. Instruments used for pitch, bank, and power control, and how those instruments are used to maintain altitude, heading, and airspeed.
   c. Trim procedure.

2. Exhibits instructional knowledge of common errors related to straight-and-level flight solely by reference to instruments by describing:

   a. "Fixation," "omission," and "emphasis" errors during instrument cross-check.
   b. Improper instrument interpretation.
   c. Improper control applications.
   d. Failure to establish proper pitch, bank, or power adjustments during altitude, heading, or airspeed corrections.
   e. Faulty trim procedure.

3. Demonstrates and simultaneously explains straight-and-level flight, solely by reference to instruments, from an instructional standpoint.
4. Analyzes and corrects simulated common errors related to straight-and-level flight, solely by reference to instruments.

Task B: *Constant Airspeed Climbs (ASEL and ASES)*

References: FAA-H-8083-3, FAA-H-8083-15, FAA-S-ACS-6.

Objective: To determine that the applicant:

1. Exhibits instructional knowledge of the elements of straight and turning, constant airspeed climbs, solely by reference to instruments by describing:

    a. Instrument cross-check, instrument interpretation, and aircraft control.
    b. instruments used for pitch, bank, and power control during entry, during the climb, and during level off, and how those instruments are used to maintain climb heading and airspeed.
    c. Trim procedure.

2. Exhibits instructional knowledge of common errors related to straight and turning, constant airspeed climbs, solely by reference to instruments by describing:

    a. "Fixation," "omission," and "emphasis" errors during instrument cross-check.
    b. Improper instrument interpretation.
    c. Improper control applications.
    d. Failure to establish proper pitch, bank, or power adjustments during heading and airspeed corrections.
    e. Improper entry or level-off procedure.
    f. Faulty trim procedure.

3. Demonstrates and simultaneously explains a straight and turning, constant airspeed climb, solely by reference to instruments, from an instructional standpoint.
4. Analyzes and corrects simulated common errors related to straight and turning, constant airspeed climbs, solely by reference to instruments.

Task C: Constant Airspeed Descents (ASEL and ASES)

References: FAA-H-8083-3, FAA-H-8083-15, FAA-S-ACS-6.

Objective: To determine that the applicant:

1. Exhibits instructional knowledge of the elements of straight and turning, constant airspeed descents, solely by reference to instruments by describing:

    a. Instrument cross-check, instrument interpretation, and aircraft control.
    b. instruments used for pitch, bank, and power control during entry, during the descent, and during level off, and how those instruments are used to maintain descent heading and airspeed.
    c. Trim procedure.

2. Exhibits instructional knowledge of common errors related to straight and turning, constant airspeed descents, solely by reference to instruments by describing:

   a. "Fixation," "omission," and "emphasis" errors during instrument cross-check.
   b. Improper instrument interpretation.
   c. Improper control applications.
   d. Failure to establish proper pitch, bank, or power adjustments during heading and airspeed corrections.
   e. Improper entry or level-off procedure.
   f. Faulty trim procedure.

3. Demonstrates and simultaneously explains a straight and turning, constant airspeed descent, solely by reference to instruments, from an instructional standpoint.
4. Analyzes and corrects simulated common errors related to straight and turning, constant airspeed descents, solely by reference to instruments.

Task D: Turns to Headings (ASEL and ASES)

References: FAA-H-8083-3, FAA-H-8083-15, FAA-S-ACS-6.

Objective: To determine that the applicant:

1. Exhibits instructional knowledge of the elements of turns to headings, solely by reference to instruments by describing:

   a. Instrument cross-check, instrument interpretation, and aircraft control.
   b. Instruments used for pitch, bank, and power control during turn entry, during the turn, and during the turn rollout, and how those instruments are used.
   c. Trim procedure.

2. Exhibits instructional knowledge of common errors related to turns to headings, solely by reference to instruments by describing:

   a. "Fixation," "omission," and "emphasis" errors during instrument cross-check.
   b. Improper instrument interpretation.
   c. Improper control applications.
   d. Failure to establish proper pitch, bank, and power adjustments during altitude, bank, and airspeed corrections.
   e. Improper entry or rollout procedure.
   f. Faulty trim procedure.

3. Demonstrates and simultaneously explains a turn to a heading, solely by reference to instruments, from an instructional standpoint.
4. Analyzes and corrects simulated common errors related to turns to headings, solely by reference to instruments.

Task E: Recovery from Unusual Flight Attitudes (ASEL and ASES)

References: FAA-H-8083-3, FAA-H-8083-15, FAA-S-ACS-6.

Objective: To determine that the applicant:

1. Exhibits instructional knowledge of the elements of recovery from unusual flight attitudes by describing:

   a. Conditions and situations that may result in unusual flight attitudes.
   b. The two basic unusual flight attitudes—nose-high (climbing turn) and nose-low (diving spiral).
   c. How unusual flight attitudes are recognized.
   d. Control sequence for recovery from a nose-high attitude and the reasons for that sequence.
   e. Control sequence for recovery from a nose-low attitude and the reasons for that sequence.
   f. Reasons why the controls should be coordinated during unusual flight attitude recoveries.

2. Exhibits instructional knowledge of common errors related to recovery from unusual flight attitudes by describing:

   a. Failure to recognize an unusual flight attitude.
   b. Consequences of attempting to recover from an unusual flight attitude by "feel" rather than by instrument indications.
   c. Inappropriate control applications during recovery.
   d. Failure to recognize from instrument indications when the airplane is passing through a level flight attitude.

3. Demonstrates and simultaneously explains a recovery from nose-high and a nose-low flight attitude from an instructional standpoint.
4. Analyzes and corrects simulated common errors related to recovery from unusual flight attitudes.

XIII. Emergency Operations

Note: *The examiner must select at least Tasks A and B.*

Task A: *Emergency Approach and Landing (Simulated) (ASEL and ASES)*

Note: *The examiner must NOT simulate a power failure by placing the fuel selector in the "off" position or by placing the mixture control in the "idle-cutoff" position. No simulated emergency approach is to be continued below 500 feet AGL, unless over an area where a safe landing can be accomplished in compliance with 14 CFR part 91, section 91.119.*

References: FAA-H-8083-3, FAA-S-8081-12, FAA-S-ACS-6; POH/AFM.

Objective: To determine that the applicant:

1. Exhibits instructional knowledge of the elements related to an emergency approach and landing by describing:

    a. Prompt establishment of the best glide airspeed and the recommended configuration.
    b. How to select a suitable emergency landing area.
    c. Planning and execution of approach to the selected landing area.
    d. Use of emergency checklist.
    e. Importance of attempting to determine reason for the malfunction.
    f. Importance of dividing attention between flying the approach and accomplishing emergency checklist.
    g. Procedures that can be used to compensate for under-shooting or overshooting selected emergency landing area.

2. Exhibits instructional knowledge of common errors related to an emergency approach and landing by describing:

    a. Improper airspeed control.
    b. Poor judgment in the selection of an emergency landing area.
    c. Failure to estimate the approximate wind speed and direction.
    d. Failure to fly the most suitable pattern for existing situation.
    e. Failure to accomplish the emergency checklist.
    f. Undershooting or overshooting selected emergency landing area.

3. Demonstrates and simultaneously explains an emergency approach with a simulated engine failure from an instructional standpoint.
4. Analyzes and corrects simulated common errors related to an emergency approach with a simulated engine failure.

Task B: Systems and Equipment Malfunctions (ASEL and ASES)

References: FAA-H-8083-3, FAA-S-8081-12, FAA-S-ACS-6; POH/AFM.

Note: *The examiner must not simulate a system or equipment malfunction in a manner that may jeopardize safe flight or result in possible damage to the airplane.*

Objective: To determine that the applicant exhibits instructional knowledge of at least five (5) of the equipment malfunctions, appropriate to the airplane used for the practical test by describing recommended pilot action for:

1. Smoke, fire, or both, during ground or flight operations.
2. Rough running engine or partial power loss.
3. Loss of engine oil pressure.
4. Fuel starvation.
5. Engine overheat.
6. Hydraulic malfunction.
7. Electrical malfunction.
8. Carburetor or induction icing.
9. Door or window opening in flight.
10. Inoperative or "runaway" trim.
11. Landing gear or flap malfunction.
12. Pressurization malfunction.

Task C: Emergency Equipment and Survival Gear (ASEL and ASES)

References: FAA-H-8083-3, FAA-S-8081-12, FAA-S-ACS-6, POH/AFM.

Objective: To determine that the applicant exhibits instructional knowledge of the elements related to emergency equipment and survival gear appropriate to the airplane used for the practical test by describing:

1. Equipment and gear appropriate for operation in various climates, over various types of terrain, and over water.
2. Purpose, method of operation or use, servicing and storage of appropriate equipment.

Task D: Emergency Descent (ASEL and ASES)

References: *FAA-H-8083-3, FAA-S-8081-12, FAA-S-ACS-6;*
POH/AFM.

Objective: To determine that the applicant exhibits instructional
knowledge of the elements related to emergency
descents appropriate to the airplane flown by:

1. Exhibiting instructional knowledge of the elements related
   to an emergency descent by describing:

   a. Situations that require an emergency descent.
   b. Proper use of the prescribed emergency checklist to
      verify accomplishment of procedures before initiating
      and during the emergency descent.
   c. Proper use of clearing procedures before initiating and
      during the emergency descent.
   d. Procedures for recovering from an emergency descent.
   e. Manufacturer's procedures.

2. Exhibiting instructional knowledge of common errors related
   to an emergency descent by describing:

   a. The consequences of failing to identify reason for
      executing an emergency descent.
   b. Improper use of the prescribed emergency checklist to
      verify accomplishment of procedures for initiating the
      emergency descent.
   c. Improper use of clearing procedures for initiating the
      emergency descent.
   d. Improper procedures for recovering from an
      emergency descent.

3. Demonstrates and simultaneously explains emergency
   descents from an instructional standpoint.
4. Analyzes and corrects simulated common errors related to
   emergency descents.

XIV. Postflight Procedures

Note: *The examiner must select Task A and, for ASES applicants,*
at least one other Task.

Task A: Postflight Procedures (ASEL and ASES)

References: *FAA-H-8083-3, FAA-H-8083-23, FAA-S-8081-12,*
FAA-S-ACS-6; POH/AFM.

Objective: To determine that the applicant:

1. Exhibits instructional knowledge of the elements of Postflight procedures by describing:

   a. Parking procedure (ASEL).
   b. Engine shutdown and securing cockpit.
   c. Deplaning passengers.
   d. Securing airplane.
   e. Postflight inspection.
   f. Refueling.

2. Exhibits instructional knowledge of common errors related to postflight procedures by describing:

   a. Hazards resulting from failure to follow recommended procedures.
   b. poor planning, improper procedure, or faulty judgment in performance of postflight procedures.

Task B: Anchoring (ASES)

References: FAA-H-8083-3, FAA-H-8083-23, FAA-S-8081-12, FAA-S-ACS-6; POH/AFM.

Objective: To determine that the applicant:

1. Exhibits instructional knowledge of the elements of anchoring by describing:

   a. How to select a suitable area for anchoring.
   b. Recommended procedure for anchoring in a lake, river, or tidal area.
   c. Number of anchors and lines to be used to ensure seaplane security in various conditions.
   d. Hazards to be avoided during anchoring.
   e. Requirements for anchoring lights.

2. Exhibits instructional knowledge of common errors related to anchoring by describing:

   a. Hazards resulting from failure to follow recommended anchoring procedures.
   b. Consequences of poor planning, improper procedure, or poor judgment when anchoring.
   c. Consequences of failure to use anchor lines of adequate length and strength to ensure seaplane security.

3. Demonstrates and simultaneously explains anchoring from an instructional standpoint.
4. Analyzes and corrects simulated common errors related to anchoring.

Task C: Docking and Mooring (ASES)

References: FAA-H-8083-3, FAA-H-8083-23, FAA-S-8081-12, FAA-S-ACS-6; POH/AFM.

Objective: To determine that the applicant:

1.   Exhibits instructional knowledge of the elements of docking and mooring by describing:

   a.   How to select a suitable area for docking and mooring.
   b.   Recommended procedure for mooring in a lake, river, or tidal area.
   c.   Number of tie-downs and lines to be used to ensure seaplane security in various conditions.
   d.   Hazards to be avoided during docking and mooring.
   e.   Requirements for docking and mooring lights.

2.   Exhibits instructional knowledge of common errors related to docking and mooring by describing:

   a.   Hazards resulting from failure to follow recommended procedures.
   b.   Consequences of poor planning, improper procedure, or poor judgment when docking and mooring.
   c.   Consequences of failure to use docking or mooring lines of adequate length and strength to ensure seaplane security.

3.   Demonstrates and simultaneously explains docking and mooring from an instructional standpoint.
4.   Analyzes and corrects simulated common errors related to docking and mooring.

Task D: Beaching (ASES)

References: FAA-H-8083-3, FAA-H-8083-23, FAA-S-8081-12, FAA-S-ACS-6; POH/AFM.

Objective: To determine that the applicant:

1.   Exhibits instructional knowledge of the elements of beaching by describing:

   a.   Recommended procedures for beaching.
   b.   Factors to be considered, such as beach selection, water depth, current, tide, and wind.
   c.   Procedures to be followed to ensure seaplane security.
   d.   Hazards to be avoided.

2. Exhibits instructional knowledge of common errors related to beaching by describing:

   a. Hazards resulting from failure to follow recommended procedures.
   b. Consequences of poor beach selection, poor planning, improper procedure, or faulty judgment when beaching.
   c. A consequence of failure to take appropriate precautions to avoid hazards or to ensure that seaplane is secure.

3. Demonstrates and simultaneously explains beaching from an instructional standpoint.
4. Analyzes and corrects simulated common errors related to beaching.

Task E: Ramping (ASES)

References: FAA-H-8083-3, FAA-H-8083-23, FAA-S-8081-12, FAA-S-ACS-6; POH/AFM.

Objective: To determine that the applicant:

1. Exhibits instructional knowledge of the elements of ramping by describing:

   a. Factors such as type of ramp surface, wind, current, and direction and control of approach speed.
   b. Recommended procedures for ramping.
   c. Hazards to be avoided.

2. Exhibits instructional knowledge of common errors related to ramping by describing:

   a. Hazards resulting from failure to follow recommended procedures.
   b. Consequences of poor planning, improper procedure, or faulty judgment when ramping.
   c. Consequences of failure to take appropriate precautions to avoid hazards or to ensure that the seaplane is secure.

3. Demonstrates and simultaneously explains ramping from an instructional standpoint.
4. Analyzes and corrects simulated common errors related to ramping.

(this page intentionally left blank)

Section 2:

Flight Instructor – Airplane

Multiengine

(this page intentionally left blank)

Additional Rating Task Table: Multiengine Airplane

Addition of a multiengine class rating (and an airplane category rating, if appropriate) to a flight instructor certificate.

Required Area of Operation	Flight Instructor Certificate and Rating(s) Held					
	ASE	RH	RG	G	IA	IH
I	None	None	None	None	None	None
II	B,M	B,D,E, M	B,D,E, M	B,D,E, M	B,D,E, M	B,D,E, M
III	None	C,D	C,D	C,D	All	All
IV	None	None	None	None	None	None
V	*	*	*	*	*	*
VI	None	*	None	*	*	*
VII	*	*	*	*	*	*
VIII	None	*	*	*	*	*
IX	*	*	*	*	*	*
X	None	*	*	*	*	*
XI	*	*	*	*	*	*
XII	None	*	*	*	None	*
XIII	*	*	*	*	*	*
XIV	*	*	*	*	*	*
XV	None	*	*	*	*	*

* Refer to the Note under the respective Area of Operation for Task requirements.

Note: *If an applicant holds more than one rating on a flight instructor certificate and the table indicates both a "None" and a "Select One" for a particular Area of Operation, the "None" entry applies. This is logical since the applicant has satisfactorily accomplished the Area of Operation on a previous flight instructor practical test. At the discretion of the examiner, the applicant's competence in* **any** *Area of Operation may be evaluated.*

Renewal or Reinstatement of a Flight Instructor Table: Airplane Multiengine Category

Required Area of Operation	Number of Tasks
II	Task B, M, and 1 other Task
III	1
IV	1
VII	2 Takeoffs and 2 Landings
IX	1
X	1
XI	1
XIII	2
XIV	1

The Renewal or Reinstatement of one rating on a Flight Instructor Certificate renews or reinstates all privileges existing on the certificate. (14 CFR part 61, section 61.197 and section 61.199)

Applicant's Practical Test Checklist

Appointment with Inspector or Examiner

Name: _____

Date/Time: _____

ACCEPTABLE AIRCRAFT

- ☐ View-Limiting Device (if applicable)
- ☐ Aircraft Documents:
  - ☐ Airworthiness Certificate
  - ☐ Registration Certificate
  - ☐ Operating Limitations
- ☐ Aircraft Maintenance Records:
  - ☐ Airworthiness Inspections
- ☐ Pilot's Operating Handbook and FAA-Approved Airplane Flight Manual

PERSONAL EQUIPMENT

- ☐ Current Aeronautical Charts
- ☐ Computer and Plotter
- ☐ Flight Plan Form
- ☐ Flight Logs
- ☐ Current AIM
- ☐ Current Airport/Facility Directory

PERSONAL RECORDS

- ☐ Pilot Certificate
- ☐ Medical Certificate
- ☐ Completed FAA Form 8710-1, Airman Certificate and/or Rating Application
- ☐ Airman Knowledge Test Report
- ☐ Logbook with Instructor's Endorsement
- ☐ Letter of Discontinuance (if applicable)
- ☐ Notice of Disapproval (if applicable)
- ☐ Approved School Graduation Certificate (if applicable)
- ☐ Examiner's Fee (if applicable)

(this page intentionally left blank)

Examiner's Practical Test Checklist

Flight Instructor – Airplane

(Multiengine)

Applicant's Name: _____

Examiner's Name: _____

Date: _____   **Type Check:** _____

Type Airplane: _____

Area of Operation:

I. FUNDAMENTALS OF INSTRUCTING
- ☐ **A.** Human Behavior and Effective Communication
- ☐ **B.** The Learning Process
- ☐ **C.** The Teaching Process
- ☐ **D.** Assessment and Critique
- ☐ **E.** Instructor Responsibilities and Professionalism
- ☐ **F.** Techniques of Flight Instruction
- ☐ **G.** Risk Management

II. TECHNICAL SUBJECT AREAS
- ☐ **A.** Aeromedical Factors
- ☐ **B.** Runway Incursion Avoidance
- ☐ **C.** Visual Scanning and Collision Avoidance
- ☐ **D.** Principles of Flight
- ☐ **E.** Airplane Flight Controls
- ☐ **F.** Airplane Weight and Balance
- ☐ **G.** Navigation and Flight Planning
- ☐ **H.** Night Operations
- ☐ **I.** High Altitude Operations
- ☐ **J.** 14 CFR and Publications
- ☐ **K.** National Airspace System
- ☐ **L.** Navigation Systems and Radar Services
- ☐ **M.** Logbook Entries and Certificate Endorsements
- ☐ **N.** Water and Seaplane Characteristics
- ☐ **O.** Seaplane Bases, Rules, and Aids to Marine Navigation

III. PREFLIGHT PREPARATION
- ☐ **A.** Certificates and Documents
- ☐ **B.** Weather Information
- ☐ **C.** Operation of Systems
- ☐ **D.** Performance and Limitations

FAA-S-8081-6D

    ☐   **E.** Airworthiness Requirements

IV. PREFLIGHT LESSON ON A MANEUVER TO BE PERFORMED IN FLIGHT

    ☐   **A.** Maneuver Lesson

V. PREFLIGHT PROCEDURES

    ☐   **A.** Preflight Inspection

    ☐   **B.** Cockpit Management

    ☐   **C.** Engine Starting

    ☐   **D.** Taxiing—Landplane

    ☐   **E.** Taxiing—Seaplane

    ☐   **F.** Sailing

    ☐   **G.** Before Takeoff Check

VI. AIRPORT AND SEAPLANE BASE OPERATIONS

    ☐   **A.** Radio Communications and ATC Light Signals

    ☐   **B.** Traffic Patterns

    ☐   **C.** Airport/Seaplane Base, Runway and Taxiway Signs, Markings, and Lighting

VII. TAKEOFFS, LANDINGS, AND GO-AROUNDS

    ☐   **A.** Normal and Crosswind Takeoff and Climb

    ☐   **B.** Short-Field (Confined Area (AMES)) Takeoff and Maximum Performance Climb

    ☐   **C.** Glassy-Water Takeoff and Climb

    ☐   **D.** Rough-Water Takeoff and Climb

    ☐   **E.** Normal and Crosswind Approach and Landing

    ☐   **F.** Go-Around/Rejected Landing

    ☐   **G.** Short-Field (Confined Area (AMES)) Approach and Landing

    ☐   **H.** Glassy-Water Approach and Landing

    ☐   **I.** Rough-Water Approach and Landing

VIII. FUNDAMENTALS OF FLIGHT

    ☐   **A.** Straight-and-Level Flight

    ☐   **B.** Level Turns

    ☐   **C.** Straight Climbs and Climbing Turns

    ☐   **D.** Straight Descents and Descending Turns

IX. PERFORMANCE MANEUVERS

    ☐   **A.** Steep Turns

X. GROUND REFERENCE MANEUVERS

    ☐   **A.** Rectangular Course

    ☐   **B.** S-Turns Across a Road

    ☐   **C.** Turns Around a Point

XI. SLOW FLIGHT AND STALLS

    ☐ **A.** Maneuvering During Slow Flight
    ☐ **B.** Power-On Stalls (Proficiency)
    ☐ **C.** Power-Off Stalls (Proficiency)
    ☐ **D.** Accelerated Maneuver Stalls (Demonstration)

XII. BASIC INSTRUMENT MANEUVERS
    ☐ **A.** Straight-and-Level Flight
    ☐ **B.** Constant Airspeed Climbs
    ☐ **C.** Constant Airspeed Descents
    ☐ **D.** Turns to Headings
    ☐ **E.** Recovery from Unusual Flight Attitudes

XIII. EMERGENCY OPERATIONS
    ☐ **A.** Systems and Equipment Malfunctions
    ☐ **B.** Engine Failure During Takeoff Before VMC
    ☐ **C.** Engine Failure After Lift-Off
    ☐ **D.** Approach and Landing with an Inoperative Engine
    ☐ **E.** Emergency Descent
    ☐ **F.** Emergency Equipment and Survival Gear

XIV. MULTIENGINE OPERATIONS
    ☐ **A.** Operation of Systems
    ☐ **B.** Performance and Limitations
    ☐ **C.** Flight Principles—Engine Inoperative
    ☐ **D.** Maneuvering with One Engine Inoperative
    ☐ **E.** V_{MC} Demonstration
    ☐ **F.** Demonstrating the Effects of Various Airspeeds and Configurations During Engine Inoperative Performance

XV. POSTFLIGHT PROCEDURES
    ☐ **A.** Postflight Procedures
    ☐ **B.** Anchoring
    ☐ **C.** Docking and Mooring
    ☐ **D.** Beaching
    ☐ **E.** Ramping

(this page intentionally left blank)

Areas of Operation:

I.   Fundamentals of Instructing

Note: *The examiner shall select Task E and one other Task.*

Task A: *Human Behavior and Effective Communication*

Reference: *FAA-H-8083-9A.*

Objective: To determine that the applicant exhibits instructional knowledge of human behavior and effective communication and how these impact effective learning by describing:

1.   Definitions of human behavior.
2.   Human needs and motivation.
3.   Defense mechanisms.
4.   Student emotional reactions.
5.   Basic elements of communication.
6.   Barriers to effective communication.
7.   Developing communication skills.

Task B: *The Learning Process*

Reference: *FAA-H-8083-9A.*

Objective: To determine that the applicant exhibits instructional knowledge of the learning process by describing:

1.   Learning theory.
2.   Perceptions and insight.
3.   Acquiring knowledge.
4.   The laws of learning.
5.   Domains of learning.
6.   Characteristics of learning.
7.   Acquiring skill knowledge.
8.   Types of practice.
9.   Scenario-based training.
10.   Errors.
11.   Memory and forgetting.
12.   Retention of learning.
13.   Transfer of learning.

Task C: *The Teaching Process*

Reference: *FAA-H-8083-9A.*

Objective: To determine that the applicant exhibits instructional knowledge of the teaching process by describing:

1. Preparation of a lesson.
2. Organization of material.
3. Training delivery methods:

   a. Lecture method.
   b. Guided discussion method.
   c. Computer assisted learning method.
   d. Demonstration-performance method.
   e. Drill and practice method.

4. Problem based learning.
5. Instruction aids and training technologies.

Task D: Assessment and Critique

Reference: *FAA-H-8083-9A.*

Objective: To determine that the applicant exhibits instructional knowledge of assessments and critiques by describing:

1. Assessment:

   a. Purpose of assessment.
   b. General characteristics of effective assessment.
   c. Traditional assessment.
   d. Authentic assessment.
   e. Oral assessment.
   f. Characteristics of effective questions.
   g. Types of questions to avoid.

2. Critique:

   a. Instructors/student critique.
   b. Student-lead critique.
   c. Small group critique.
   d. Individual student critique by another student.
   e. Self-critique.
   f. Written critique.

Task E: Instructor Responsibilities and Professionalism

Reference: *FAA-H-8083-9A.*

Objective: To determine that the applicant exhibits instructional knowledge of instructor responsibilities and professionalism by describing:

1. Aviation instructor responsibilities:

    a. Helping students learn.
    b. Providing adequate instruction.
    c. Standards of performance.
    d. Minimizing student frustrations.

2. Flight instructor responsibilities:

    a. Physiological obstacles for flight students.
    b. Ensuring student ability.
    c. Professionalism.
    d. Evaluation of student ability.
    e. Aviation instructors and exams.
    f. Professional development.

Task F: Techniques of Flight Instruction

Reference: FAA-H-8083-9A.

Objective: To determine that the applicant exhibits instructional knowledge of instructor responsibilities and professionalism by describing:

1. Obstacles to learning during flight instruction.
2. Demonstration-performance training delivery.
3. Positive exchange of controls.
4. Sterile cockpit.
5. Use of distractions.
6. Integrated flight instruction.
7. Assessment of piloting ability.
8. Aeronautical decision making.

Task G: Risk Management

Reference: FAA-H-8083-9A.

Objective: To determine that the applicant exhibits instructional knowledge of risk management by describing:

1. Principles of risk management.
2. Risk management process.
3. Level of risk.
4. Assessing risk.
5. Mitigating risk.
6. IMSAFE checklist.
7. PAVE checklist.
8. 5P checklist.

II.   Technical Subject Areas

Note: *The examiner must select Tasks B, M, and at least one other Task.*

Task A: *Aeromedical Factors*

References: AIM; FAA-H-8083-3, FAA-S-8081-12, FAA-S-ACS-6.

Objective: To determine that the applicant exhibits instructional knowledge of the elements related to aeromedical factors by describing:

1.   How to obtain an appropriate medical certificate.
2.   How to obtain a medical certificate in the event of a possible medical deficiency.
3.   The causes, symptoms, effects, and corrective action of the following medical factors:

   a.   hypoxia.
   b.   hyperventilation.
   c.   middle ear and sinus problems.
   d.   spatial disorientation.
   e.   motion sickness.
   f.   carbon monoxide poisoning.
   g.   fatigue and stress.
   h.   dehydration.

4.   The effects of alcohol and drugs, and their relationship to flight safety.
5.   The effect of nitrogen excesses during scuba dives and how this affects pilots and passengers during flight.

Task B: *Runway Incursion Avoidance*

References: AC 91-73, A/FD, AIM; FAA-H-8083-2, FAA-H-8083-3, FAA-H-8083-25.

Note: *If this task has been previously performed in the aircraft during an earlier instructor rating, the determination of the required knowledge can be demonstrated during the brief, at the discretion of the examiner.*

Objective: To determine that the applicant exhibits instructional knowledge of the elements of runway incursion avoidance by describing:

1.   Distinct challenges and requirements during taxi operations not found in other phases of flight operations.

2. Procedures for appropriate cockpit activities during taxiing including taxi route planning, briefing the location of hot spots, (can be found in AFD) communicating and coordinating with ATC.
3. Procedures for steering, maneuvering, maintaining taxiway, runway position, and situational awareness.
4. The relevance/importance of hold lines.
5. Procedures for ensuring the pilot maintains strict focus to the movement of the aircraft and ATC communications, including the elimination of all distractive activities (i.e. cell phone, texting, conversations with passengers) during aircraft taxi, takeoff and climb out to cruise altitude.
6. Procedures for holding the pilot's workload to a minimum during taxi operations.
7. Taxi operation planning procedures, such as recording taxi instructions, reading back taxi clearances, and reviewing taxi routes on the airport diagram,
8. Procedures for ensuring that clearance or instructions that are actually received are adhered to rather than the ones expected to be received.
9. Procedures for maintaining/enhancing situational awareness when conducting taxi operations in relation to other aircraft operations in the vicinity as well as to other vehicles moving on the airport.
10. Procedures for briefing if a landing rollout to a taxiway exit will place the pilot in close proximity to another runway which can result in a runway incursion.
11. Appropriate after landing/taxi procedures in the event the aircraft is on a taxiway that is between parallel runways.
12. Specific procedures for operations at an airport with an operating air traffic control tower, with emphasis on ATC communications and runway entry/crossing authorizations.
13. ATC communications and pilot actions before takeoff, before landing, and after landing at towered and non-towered airports.
14. Procedures unique to night operations.
15. Operations at non-towered airports.
16. Use of aircraft exterior lighting.
17. Low visibility operations.

Task C: *Visual Scanning and Collision Avoidance*

References: AC 90-48, AIM; FAA-H-8083-3, FAA-H-8083-25.

Objective: To determine that the applicant exhibits instructional knowledge of the elements of visual scanning and collision avoidance by describing:

1. Relationship between a pilot's physical condition and vision.

2. Environmental conditions that degrade vision.
3. Vestibular and visual illusions.
4. "See and avoid" concept.
5. Proper visual scanning procedure.
6. Relationship between poor visual scanning habits and increased collision risk.
7. Proper clearing procedures.
8. Importance of knowing aircraft blind spots.
9. Relationship between aircraft speed differential and collision risk.
10. Situations which involve the greatest collision risk.

Task D: Principles of Flight

References: FAA-H-8083-3, FAA-H-8083-25.

Objective: To determine that the applicant exhibits instructional knowledge of the elements of principles of flight by describing:

1. Airfoil design characteristics.
2. Airplane stability and controllability.
3. Turning tendency (torque effect).
4. Load factors in airplane design.
5. Wingtip vortices and precautions to be taken.

Task E: Airplane Flight Controls

References: FAA-H-8083-3, FAA-H-8083-25.

Objective: To determine that the applicant exhibits instructional knowledge of the elements related to the airplane flight controls by describing the purpose, location, direction of movement, effect and proper procedure for use of the:

1. Primary flight controls.
2. Trim control(s).
3. Wing flaps.

Task F: Airplane Weight and Balance

References: FAA-H-8083-1, FAA-H-8083-3, FAA-H-8083-25, FAA-S-8081-12, FAA-S-ACS-6.

Objective: To determine that the applicant exhibits instructional knowledge of the elements of airplane weight and balance by describing:

1. Weight and balance terms.

2. Effect of weight and balance on performance.
3. Methods of weight and balance control.
4. Determination of total weight and center of gravity and the changes that occur when adding, removing, or shifting weight.

Task G: Navigation and Flight Planning

References: FAA-H-8083-3, FAA-H-8083-25, FAA-S-8081-12, FAA-S-ACS-6.

Objective: To determine that the applicant exhibits instructional knowledge of the elements of navigation and flight planning by describing:

1. Terms used in navigation.
2. Features of aeronautical charts.
3. Importance of using the proper and current aeronautical charts.
4. Method of plotting a course, selection of fuel stops and alternates, and appropriate actions in the event of unforeseen situations.
5. Fundamentals of pilotage and dead reckoning.
6. Fundamentals of radio navigation.
7. Diversion to an alternate.
8. Lost procedures.
9. Computation of fuel consumption.
10. Importance of preparing and properly using a flight log.
11. Importance of a weather check and the use of good judgment in making a "go/no-go" decision.
12. Purpose of, and procedure used in, filing a flight plan.
13. Global positioning system (GPS) navigation.

Task H: Night Operations

References: AIM; FAA-H-8083-3, FAA-H-8083-25, FAA-S-8081-12, FAA-S-ACS-6.

Objective: To determine that the applicant exhibits instructional knowledge of the elements of night operations by describing:

1. Factors related to night vision.
2. Disorientation and night optical illusions.
3. Proper adjustment of interior lights.
4. Importance of having a flashlight with a red lens.
5. Night preflight inspection.
6. Engine starting procedures, including use of position and anti-collision lights prior to start.

7. Taxiing and orientation on an airport.
8. Takeoff and climb-out.
9. In-flight orientation.
10. Importance of verifying the airplane's attitude by reference to flight instruments.
11. Night emergency procedures.
12. Traffic patterns.
13. Approaches and landings with and without landing lights.
14. Go-arounds.

Task I: High Altitude Operations

References: *14 CFR part 91, AC 61-107, AIM; FAA-H-8083-3, FAA-S-8081-12; POH/AFM.*

Objective: To determine that the applicant exhibits instructional knowledge of the elements of high altitude operations by describing:

1. Regulatory requirements for use of oxygen.
2. Physiological hazards associated with high altitude operations.
3. Characteristics of a pressurized airplane and various types of supplemental oxygen systems.
4. Importance of "aviator's breathing oxygen."
5. Care and storage of high-pressure oxygen bottles.
6. Problems associated with rapid decompression and corresponding solutions.

Task J: 14 CFR and Publications

References: *14 CFR parts 1, 61, 91; AIM, NTSB part 830, FAA-H-8083-25, POH/AFM.*

Objective: To determine that the applicant exhibits instructional knowledge of the elements related to the Code of Federal Regulations and related publications by describing:

1. Availability and method of revision of 14 CFR parts 1, 61, 91, and NTSB part 830:

   a. purpose.
   b. general content.

2. Availability of flight information publications, advisory circulars, practical test standards, pilot operating handbooks, and FAA-approved airplane flight manuals by describing:

    a. availability.
    b. purpose.
    c. general content.

Task K: National Airspace System

References: 14 CFR part 91, AIM; FAA-S-8081-12, FAA-S-ACS-6.

Objective: To determine that the applicant exhibits instructional knowledge of the elements of the national airspace system by describing:

1. Basic VFR weather minimums—for all classes of airspace.
2. Airspace classes—their operating rules, pilot certification, and airplane equipment requirements for the following:

    a. Class A.
    b. Class B.
    c. Class C.
    d. Class D.
    e. Class E.
    f. Class G.

3. Special use airspace (SUA).
4. Temporary flight restrictions (TFR).

Task L: Navigation Aids and Radar Services

References: AIM; FAA-H-8083-3, FAA-H-8083-15, FAA-S-8081-12, FAA-S-ACS-6.

Objective: To determine that the applicant exhibits instructional knowledge of the elements related to navigation aids and radar service by describing:

1. One ground-based navigational aid (VOR/VORTAC, NDB, and DME).
2. Satellite-based navigation aids.
3. Radar service and procedures.

Task M: Logbook Entries and Certificate Endorsements

References: 14 CFR part 61; AC 61-65.

Objective: To determine that the applicant exhibits instructional knowledge of the elements related to logbook entries and certificate endorsements by describing:

1. Required logbook entries for instruction given.
2. Required student pilot certificate endorsements, including appropriate logbook entries.
3. Preparation of a recommendation for a pilot practical test, including appropriate logbook entry for:

   a. initial pilot certification.
   b. additional pilot certification
   c. additional aircraft qualification.

4. Required endorsement of a pilot logbook for the satisfactory completion of the required FAA flight review.
5. Required flight instructor records.

Task N: *Water and Seaplane Characteristics (AMES)*

References: FAA-H-8083-3, FAA-H-8083-23, FAA-S-8081-12, FAA-S-ACS-6; Seaplane Manual.

Objective: To determine that the applicant exhibits instructional knowledge of the elements related to water and seaplane characteristics by describing:

1. The characteristics of water surface as affected by features, such as:

   a. size and location of water operating area.
   b. protected and unprotected operating areas.
   c. surface wind.
   d. direction and height of waves.
   e. direction and strength of water current.
   f. floating and partially submerged debris.
   g. sandbars, islands, and shoals.

2. Seaplane float or hull construction and its relationship to performance.
3. Causes of porpoising and skipping and pilot action necessary to prevent or to correct those occurrences.

Task O: *Seaplane Bases, Rules, and Aids to Marine Navigation (AMES)*

References: 14 CFR part 91; AC 61-69, FAA-H-8083-3, FAA-H-8083-23, FAA-S-8081-12, FAA-S-ACS-6; USCG Navigation Rules, International-Inland.

Objective: To determine that the applicant exhibits instructional knowledge of the elements related to seaplane bases, rules, and aids to marine navigation by describing:

1. How to locate and identify seaplane bases on charts or in directories.
2. Operating restrictions at various seaplane bases.
3. Right-of-way, steering, and sailing rules pertinent to seaplane operation.
4. Purpose and identification of marine navigation aids such as buoys, beacons, lights, and sound signals.

III. Preflight Preparation

Note: *The examiner must select at least one Task.*

Task A: *Certificates and Documents*

References: *14 CFR parts 23, 43, 61, 91; FAA-H-8083-3, FAA-H-8083-25, FAA-S-8081-12, FAA-S-ACS-6; POH/AFM.*

Objective: To determine that the applicant exhibits instructional knowledge of the elements related to certificates and documents by describing:

1. The training requirements for the issuance of recreational, private, and commercial pilot certificates.
2. The privileges and limitations of pilot certificates and ratings at recreational, private, and commercial levels.
3. Class and duration of medical certificates.
4. Recent pilot flight experience requirements.
5. Required entries in pilot logbook or flight record.

Task B: *Weather Information*

References: *AC 00-6, AC 00-45; FAA-H-8083-25, FAA-S-8081-12, FAA-S-ACS-6.*

Objective: To determine that the applicant exhibits instructional knowledge of the elements related to weather information by describing:

1. Importance of a thorough preflight weather briefing.
2. Means and sources of obtaining weather information.
3. Use of real-time weather reports, forecasts, and charts for developing scenario-based training.
4. In-flight weather advisories.
5. Recognition of aviation weather hazards to include wind shear.
6. Factors to be considered in making a "go/no-go" decision.

Task C: *Operation of Systems*

References: *FAA-H-8083-3, FAA-H-8083-23, FAA-H-8083-25, FAA-S-8081-12, FAA-S-ACS-6; POH/AFM.*

Objective: To determine that the applicant exhibits instructional knowledge of the elements related to the operation of systems, as applicable to the airplane used for the practical test, by describing the following systems:

1. Primary and secondary flight controls
2. Trim
3. Water rudders (AMES)
4. Powerplant and propeller
5. Landing gear
6. Fuel, oil, and hydraulic
7. Electrical
8. Avionics including autopilot
9. Pitot static, vacuum/pressure and associated instruments
10. Environmental
11. Deicing and anti-icing

Task D: Performance and Limitations

References: *FAA-H-8083-3, FAA-H-8083-23, FAA-H-8083-25, FAA-S-8081-12, FAA-S-ACS-6; AC 61-84; POH/AFM.*

Objective: To determine that the applicant exhibits instructional knowledge of the elements related to performance and limitations by describing:

1. Determination of weight and balance condition.
2. Use of performance charts, tables, and other data in determining performance in various phases of flight.
3. Effects of exceeding airplane limitations.
4. Effects of atmospheric conditions on performance.
5. Factors to be considered in determining that the required performance is within the airplane's capabilities.

Task E: Airworthiness Requirements

References: *14 CFR parts 39, 43; FAA-S-8081-12, FAA-S-ACS-6; POH/AFM.*

Objective: To determine that the applicant exhibits instructional knowledge of the elements related to required airworthiness by explaining:

1. Required instruments and equipment for day/night VFR.
2. Procedures and limitations for determining airworthiness of the airplane with inoperative instruments and equipment without a minimum equipment list (MEL).
3. Requirements and procedures for obtaining a special flight permit.
4. Airworthiness directives, compliance records, maintenance/ inspection requirements, and appropriate records.
5. Procedures for deferring maintenance on aircraft without an approved MEL.

IV. Preflight Lesson on a Maneuver to be Performed in Flight

Note: *Examiner must select at least one maneuver Task from Areas of Operation VII through XIV, and ask the applicant to present a preflight lesson on the selected maneuver as the lesson would be taught to a student.*

Task A: Maneuver Lesson

References: *FAA-H-8083-3, FAA-H-8083-9, FAA-H-8083-23, FAA-H-8083-25, FAA-S-8081-12, FAA-S-ACS-6; POH/AFM.*

Objective: To determine that the applicant exhibits instructional knowledge of the selected maneuver by:

1. Stating the purpose.
2. Giving an accurate, comprehensive oral description, including the elements and common errors.
3. Using instructional aids, as appropriate.
4. Describing the recognition, analysis, and correction of common errors.

V. Preflight Procedures

Note: *The examiner must select at least one Task.*

Task A: Preflight Inspection (AMEL and AMES)

References: *AC 61-84; FAA-H-8083-3, FAA-H-8083-23, FAA-S-8081-12, FAA-S-ACS-6; POH/AFM.*

Objective: To determine that the applicant:

1. Exhibits instructional knowledge of the elements of a preflight inspection, as applicable to the airplane used for the practical test, by describing:

   a. reasons for the preflight inspection, items that should be inspected, and how defects are detected.
   b. importance of using the appropriate checklist.
   c. how to determine fuel and oil quantity and contamination.
   d. detection of fuel, oil, and hydraulic leaks.
   e. inspection of the oxygen system, including supply and proper operation (if applicable).
   f. inspection of the flight controls and water rudder (if applicable).
   g. detection of visible structural damage.
   h. removal of tie-downs, control locks, and wheel chocks.
   i. removal of ice and frost.
   j. importance of the proper loading and securing of baggage, cargo, and equipment.
   k. use of sound judgment in determining whether the airplane is in an airworthy condition for safe flight.

2. Exhibits instructional knowledge of common errors related to a preflight inspection by describing:

   a. failure to use or the improper use of checklist.
   b. hazards which may result from allowing distractions to interrupt a visual inspection.
   c. inability to recognize discrepancies to determine airworthiness.
   d. failure to assure servicing with the proper fuel and oil.
   e. failure to ensure proper loading and securing of baggage, cargo, and equipment.

3. Demonstrates and simultaneously explains a preflight inspection from an instructional standpoint.

Task B: Cockpit Management (AMEL and AMES)

References: FAA-H-8083-3, FAA-S-8081-12, FAA-S-ACS-6; POH/AFM.

Objective: To determine that the applicant:

1. Exhibits instructional knowledge of the elements of cockpit management by describing:

    a. proper arranging and securing of essential materials and equipment in the cockpit.
    b. proper use and/or adjustment of cockpit items such as safety belts, shoulder harnesses, rudder pedals, and seats.
    c. occupant briefing on emergency procedures and use of safety belts.
    d. detection of fuel, oil, and hydraulic leaks.

2. Exhibits instructional knowledge of common errors related to cockpit management by describing:

    a. failure to place and secure essential materials and equipment for easy access during flight.
    b. failure to properly use and/or adjust cockpit items, such as safety belts, shoulder harnesses, rudder pedals, and seats.
    c. failure to provide improper adjustment of equipment and controls. occupant briefing on emergency procedures and use of safety belts.
    d. failure to provide occupant briefing on emergency procedures and use of safety belts.
    e. failure to ensure proper loading and securing of baggage, cargo, and equipment.

3. Demonstrates and simultaneously explains cockpit management from an instructional standpoint.

Task C: Engine Starting (AMEL and AMES)

References: AC 91-13, AC 91-55; FAA-H-8083-3, FAA-H-8083-23, FAA-H-8083-25, FAA-H-8083-3, FAA-S-8081-12, FAA-S-ACS-6; POH/AFM.

Objective: To determine that the applicant:

1. Exhibits instructional knowledge of the elements of engine starting, as appropriate to the airplane used for the practical test by describing:

    a. safety precautions related to starting.
    b. use of external power.

c. effect of atmospheric conditions on starting.
d. importance of following the appropriate checklist.
e. adjustment of engine controls during start.
f. prevention of airplane movement during and after start.

2. Exhibits instructional knowledge of common errors related to engine starting by describing:

a. failure to properly use the appropriate checklist.
b. failure to use safety precautions related to starting.
c. improper adjustment of engine controls during start.
d. failure to assure proper clearance of the propeller.

3. Demonstrates and simultaneously explains engine starting from an instructional standpoint.

Task D: Taxiing—Landplane (AMEL)

References: FAA-H-8083-3, FAA-S-8081-12, FAA-S-ACS-6; POH/AFM.

Objective: To determine that the applicant:

1. Exhibits instructional knowledge of the elements of landplane taxiing by describing:

a. proper brake check and correct use of brakes.
b. compliance with airport/taxiway surface marking, signals, and ATC clearances or instructions.
c. how to control direction and speed.
d. flight control positioning for various wind conditions.
e. procedures used to avoid other aircraft and hazards.
f. runway incursion avoidance procedures.
g. procedures for eliminating pilot distractions.
h. use of taxi chart during taxi.
i. airport, taxiway, and runway position situational awareness.
j. additional taxiing operations concerns at a non-towered airport.

2. Exhibits instructional knowledge of common errors related to landplane taxiing by describing:

a. improper use of brakes.
b. improper positioning of the flight controls for various wind conditions.
c. hazards of taxiing too fast.
d. hazards associated with failure to comply with airport/taxiway surface marking, signals, and ATC clearances or instructions.

e. hazards of taxiing at non-towered airports.

3. Demonstrates and simultaneously explains landplane taxiing from an instructional standpoint.

4. Analyzes and corrects simulated common errors related to landplane taxiing.

Task E: Taxiing—Seaplane (AMES)

References: *FAA-H-8083-3, FAA-H-8083-23, FAA-S-8081-12, FAA-S-ACS-6; POH/AFM; USCG Navigation Rules, International-Inland.*

Objective: To determine that the applicant:

1. Exhibits instructional knowledge of the elements of seaplane taxiing by describing:

   a. wind effect.
   b. prevention of porpoising and skipping.
   c. selection of the most suitable course for taxiing, following available marking aids.
   d. conditions where idle, plowing, and step taxiing are used.
   e. procedures for idle, plowing, and step taxiing.
   f. control positioning for various wind conditions.
   g. use of water rudders.
   h. procedures used to avoid other aircraft and hazards.
   i. procedures used to avoid excessive water spray into the propeller.
   j. 180° and 360° turns in idle, plowing, and step positions.
   k. application of right-of-way rules.

2. Exhibits instructional knowledge of common errors related to seaplane taxiing by describing:

   a. improper positioning of flight controls for various wind conditions.
   b. improper control of speed and direction.
   c. failure to prevent porpoising and skipping.
   d. failure to use the most suitable course and available marking aids.
   e. failure to use proper clearing procedures to avoid hazards.
   f. failure to apply right-of-way rules.

3. Demonstrates and simultaneously explains emergency descents from an instructional standpoint.

4. Analyzes and corrects simulated common errors related to emergency descents.

Task F: Sailing (AMES)

References: *FAA-H-8083-3, FAA-H-8083-23, FAA-S-8081-12, FAA-S-ACS-6; POH/AFM; USCG Navigation Rules, International-Inland.*

Objective: To determine that the applicant:

1. Exhibits instructional knowledge of the elements of sailing by describing:

   a. procedures used in sailing (engine idling or shut down, as appropriate).
   b. conditions and situations where sailing would be used.
   c. selection of the most favorable course to follow.
   d. use of flight controls, flaps, doors, and water rudders to follow the selected course.
   e. procedures used to change direction from downwind to crosswind.
   f. control of speed.

2. Exhibits instructional knowledge of common errors related to sailing by describing:

   a. failure to select the most favorable course to destination.
   b. improper use of controls, flaps, and water rudders.
   c. improper procedure when changing direction.
   d. improper procedure for speed control.

3. Demonstrates and simultaneously explains sailing from an instructional standpoint.
4. Analyzes and corrects simulated common errors related to sailing.

Task G: Before Takeoff Check (AMEL and AMES)

References: *FAA-H-8083-3, FAA-H-8083-23, FAA-S-8081-12, FAA-S-ACS-6; POH/AFM.*

Objective: To determine that the applicant:

1. Exhibits instructional knowledge of the elements of the before takeoff check by describing:

   a. positioning the airplane with consideration for other aircraft, surface conditions, and wind.

b. division of attention inside and outside the cockpit.
c. importance of following the checklist and responding to each checklist item.
d. reasons for ensuring suitable engine temperatures and pressures for run-up and takeoff.
e. method used to determine that airplane is in a safe operating condition.
f. importance of reviewing takeoff performance airspeeds, expected takeoff distances, and emergency procedures.
g. method used for ensuring that the takeoff area or path is free of hazards.
h. method of avoiding runway incursions and ensures no conflict with traffic prior to taxiing into takeoff position.

2. Exhibits instructional knowledge of common errors related to the before takeoff check by describing:

a. failure to properly use the appropriate checklist.
b. improper positioning of the airplane.
c. improper acceptance of marginal engine performance.
d. an improper check of flight controls.
e. hazards of failure to review takeoff and emergency procedures.
f. failure to avoid runway incursions and to ensure no conflict with traffic prior to taxiing into takeoff position.

3. Demonstrates and simultaneously explains a before takeoff check from an instructional standpoint.
4. Analyzes and corrects simulated common errors related to a before takeoff check.

VI.   Airport and Seaplane Base Operations

Note: *The examiner must select at least one Task.*

Task A: *Radio Communications and ATC Light Signals (AMEL and AMES)*

References: AIM; FAA-H-8083-3, FAA-H-8083-25, FAA-S-8081-12, FAA-S-ACS-6.

Objective: To determine that the applicant:

1.   Exhibits instructional knowledge of the elements of radio communications and ATC light signals by describing:

   a.   selection and use of appropriate radio frequencies.
   b.   recommended procedure and phraseology for radio communications.
   c.   Receipt of, acknowledgement of, and compliance with ATC clearances and instructions.
   d.   interpretation of, and compliance with, ATC light signals.

2.   Exhibits instructional knowledge of common errors related to radio communications and ATC light signals by describing:

   a.   use of improper frequencies.
   b.   improper procedure and phraseology when using radio communications, not stating their call sign/N#, and at non-towered airports, stating their position, runway for takeoff, and the airport of operation.
   c.   failure to acknowledge, or properly comply with, ATC clearances and instructions.
   d.   failure to understand, or to properly comply with, ATC light signals.

3.   Demonstrates and simultaneously explains radio communication procedures from an instructional standpoint.
4.   Analyzes and corrects simulated common errors related to radio communications and ATC light signals.

Task B: Traffic Patterns (AMEL and AMES)

References: AC 90-42, AC 90-66; FAA-H-8083-25, FAA-H-8083-3, FAA-S-8081-12, FAA-S-ACS-6; AIM.

Objective: To determine that the applicant:

1. Exhibits instructional knowledge of the elements of traffic patterns by describing:

   a. operations at airports and seaplane bases with and without operating control towers.
   b. adherence to traffic pattern procedures, instructions, and rules.
   c. how to maintain proper spacing from other traffic.
   d. how to maintain the desired ground track.
   e. wind shear and wake turbulence avoidance procedures.
   f. orientation with the runway or landing area in use.
   g. how to establish a final approach at an appropriate distance from the runway or landing area.
   h. use of checklist.

2. Exhibits instructional knowledge of common errors related to traffic patterns by describing:

   a. failure to comply with traffic pattern instructions, procedures, and rules.
   b. improper correction for wind drift.
   c. inadequate spacing from other traffic.
   d. poor altitude or airspeed control.

3. Demonstrates and simultaneously explains traffic patterns from an instructional standpoint.
4. Analyzes and corrects simulated common errors related to traffic patterns.

Task C: Airport/Seaplane Base, Runway and Taxiway Signs, Markings, and Lighting (AMEL and AMES)

References: AC 91-73, AC 150/5340-1, AC 150/5340-18; FAA-H-8083-23, FAA-H-8083-25, FAA-S-8081-12, FAA-S-ACS-6.

Objective: To determine that the applicant exhibits instructional knowledge of the elements of airport/seaplane base, runway and taxiway signs, markings, and lighting by describing:

1. Exhibits instructional knowledge of the elements of airport/ seaplane base, runway and taxiway signs, markings, and lighting by describing:

    a. identification and proper interpretation of airport/seaplane base, runway and taxiway signs and markings, with emphasis on runway incursion avoidance.
    b. identification and proper interpretation of airport/seaplane base, runway and taxiway lighting, with emphasis on runway incursion avoidance.

2. Exhibits instructional knowledge of common errors related to airport/seaplane base, runway and taxiway signs, markings, and lighting by describing:

    a. failure to comply with airport/seaplane base, runway and taxiway signs and markings.
    b. failure to comply with airport/seaplane base, runway and taxiway lighting.
    c. failure to use proper runway incursion avoidance procedures.

3. Demonstrates and simultaneously explains airport/seaplane base, runway and taxiway signs, markings, and lighting from an instructional standpoint.
4. Analyzes and corrects simulated common errors related to airport/seaplane base, runway and taxiway signs, markings, and lighting.

VII. Takeoffs, Landings, and Go-Arounds

Note: *The examiner must select at least two takeoff and two landing Tasks.*

Task A: *Normal and Crosswind Takeoff and Climb (AMEL and AMES)*

References: FAA-H-8083-3, FAA-H-8083-23, FAA-S-8081-12, FAA-S-ACS-6; POH/AFM.

Objective: To determine that the applicant:

1.   Exhibits instructional knowledge of the elements of a normal and crosswind takeoff and climb by describing:

   a.   procedures before taxiing onto the runway or takeoff area to ensure runway incursion avoidance. Verify ATC clearance/no aircraft on final at non-towered airports before entering the runway, and ensure that you are on the correct takeoff runway positioning the airplane with consideration for other aircraft, surface conditions, and wind.
   b.   normal and crosswind takeoff procedures.
   c.   difference between a normal and a glassy-water takeoff (seaplane).
   d.   normal and crosswind lift-off procedures.
   e.   proper climb attitude, power setting, and airspeed (V_Y).
   f.   proper use of checklist.

2.   Exhibits instructional knowledge of common errors related to a normal and crosswind takeoff and climb by describing:

   a.   improper runway incursion avoidance procedures.
   b.   improper use of controls during a normal or crosswind takeoff.
   c.   inappropriate lift-off procedures.
   d.   improper climb attitude, power setting and airspeed (V_Y).
   e.   improper use of checklist.

3.   Demonstrates and simultaneously explains a normal or a crosswind takeoff and climb from an instructional standpoint.
4.   Analyzes and corrects simulated common errors related to a normal or a crosswind takeoff and climb.

Task B: Short-Field (Confined Area (AMES)) Takeoff and Maximum Performance and Climb (AMEL and AMES)

References: FAA-H-8083-3, FAA-H-8083-23, FAA-S-8081-12, FAA-S-ACS-6; POH/AFM.

Objective: To determine that the applicant:

1. Exhibits instructional knowledge of the elements of a short-field takeoff and climb by describing:

   a. procedures before taxiing onto the runway or takeoff area to ensure runway incursion avoidance. Verify ATC clearance/no aircraft on final at non-towered airports before entering the runway, and ensure that you are on the correct takeoff runway positioning the airplane with consideration for other aircraft, surface conditions, and wind.
   b. short-field takeoff procedures.
   c. short-field lift-off procedures.
   d. initial climb attitude and airspeed (V_x) until obstacle is cleared (50 feet AGL).
   e. proper use of checklist.

2. Exhibits instructional knowledge of common errors related to a short-field takeoff and climb by describing:

   a. improper runway incursion avoidance procedures.
   b. improper use of controls during a short-field takeoff.
   c. improper lift-off procedures.
   d. improper initial climb attitude, power setting, and airspeed (V_x) to clear obstacle.
   e. improper use of checklist.

3. Demonstrates and simultaneously explains a short-field takeoff and climb from an instructional standpoint.
4. Analyzes and corrects simulated common errors related to a short-field takeoff and climb.

Task C: Glassy-Water Takeoff and Climb (ASES)

References: AC 91-69; FAA-H-8083-3, FAA-H-8083-23, FAA-S-8081-12, FAA-S-ACS-6; POH/AFM.

Objective: To determine that the applicant:

1. Exhibits instructional knowledge of the elements of a glassy-water takeoff and climb by describing:

   a. procedures before taxiing onto the takeoff area to ensure waterway is clear of objects or obstructions.
   b. flight control, flap and water rudder use during glassy-water takeoff procedures.
   c. appropriate planning attitude and lift-off procedures on glassy water.
   d. initial climb attitude and airspeed (V_X, if an obstacle is present (50 feet AGL), or V_Y).
   e. proper use of after-takeoff checklist.

2. Exhibits instructional knowledge of common errors related to a glassy-water takeoff and climb by describing:

   a. improper takeoff water way clearance procedures.
   b. poor judgment in the selection of a suitable takeoff area.
   c. improper use of controls during a glassy-water takeoff.
   d. inappropriate lift-off procedures.
   e. hazards of inadvertent contact with the water after becoming airborne.
   f. improper climb attitude, power setting, and airspeed (V_Y or V_X).
   g. improper use of checklist.

3. Demonstrates and simultaneously explains a glassy-water takeoff and climb from an instructional standpoint.
4. Analyzes and corrects simulated common errors related to a glassy-water takeoff and climb.

Task D: Rough-Water Takeoff and Climb (AMES)

References: FAA-H-8083-3, FAA-H-8083-23, FAA-S-8081-12, FAA-S-ACS-6; POH/AFM.

Objective: To determine that the applicant:

1. Exhibits instructional knowledge of the elements of a rough-water takeoff and climb by describing:

   a. procedures before taxiing onto the takeoff area to ensure waterway is clear of objects or obstructions.
   b. flight control, flap, and water rudder use during rough-water takeoff procedures.
   c. appropriate planning attitude and lift-off procedures on rough water.

d.   initial climb attitude and airspeed (V_X, if an obstacle is present (50 feet AGL), or V_Y).

e.   proper use of after takeoff checklist.

2.   Exhibits instructional knowledge of common errors related to a rough-water takeoff and climb by describing:

a.   improper takeoff water way clearance procedures.

b.   poor judgment in the selection of a suitable takeoff area.

c.   improper use of controls during a rough-water takeoff.

d.   inappropriate lift-off procedures.

e.   hazards of inadvertent contact with the water after becoming airborne.

f.   improper climb attitude, power setting, and airspeed (V_Y or V_X).

g.   improper use of checklist.

3.   Demonstrates and simultaneously explains a rough-water takeoff and climb from an instructional standpoint.

4.   Analyzes and corrects simulated common errors related to a rough-water takeoff and climb.

Task E: Normal and Crosswind Approach and Landing (AMEL and AMES)

References: FAA-H-8083-3, FAA-H-8083-23, FAA-S-8081-12, FAA-S-ACS-6; POH/AFM.

Objective: To determine that the applicant:

1.   Exhibits instructional knowledge of the elements of a normal and a crosswind approach and landing by describing:

a.   how to determine landing performance and limitations.

b.   configuration, power, and trim.

c.   obstructions and other hazards which should be considered.

d.   a stabilized approach at the recommended airspeed to the selected touchdown area.

e.   course of action if selected touchdown area is going to be missed.

f.   coordination of flight controls.

g.   a precise ground track.

h.   wind shear and wake turbulence.

i.   crosswind procedure.

j.   timing, judgment, and control procedure during roundout and touchdown.

k. directional control after touchdown.
l. use of brakes (landplane).
m. use of checklist.
n. after landing runway incursion procedures.

2. Exhibits instructional knowledge of common errors related to a normal and a crosswind approach and landing by describing:

   a. improper use of landing performance data and limitations.
   b. failure to establish approach and landing configuration at appropriate time or in proper sequence.
   c. failure to establish and maintain a stabilized approach.
   d. inappropriate removal of hand from throttles.
   e. improper procedure during roundout and touchdown.
   f. poor directional control after touchdown.
   g. improper use of brakes (landplane).
   h. failure to ensure receipt and acknowledgement of landing clearance.
   i. failure to review airport diagram for runway exit situational awareness to avoid a runway incursion after landing.

3. Demonstrates and simultaneously explains a normal or a crosswind approach and landing from an instructional standpoint.
4. Analyzes and corrects simulated common errors related to a normal or crosswind approach and landing.

Task F: Go-Around/Rejected Landing (AMEL and AMES)

References: FAA-H-8083-3, FAA-H-8083-23, FAA-S-8081-12, FAA-S-ACS-6; POH/AFM.

Objective: To determine that the applicant:

1. Exhibits instructional knowledge of the elements of a go-around/rejected landing by describing:

   a. situations in which a go-around is necessary.
   b. importance of making a prompt decision.
   c. importance of applying takeoff power immediately after the go-around decision is made.
   d. importance of establishing proper pitch attitude.
   e. wing flaps retraction.
   f. use of trim.
   g. landing gear retraction.
   h. proper climb speed.
   i. proper track and obstruction clearance.

j.   use of checklist.

k.   Importance of manufacturer's recommended procedures.

2.   Exhibits instructional knowledge of common errors related to a go-around/rejected landing by describing:

a.   failure to recognize a situation where a go-around/rejected landing is necessary.

b.   hazards of delaying a decision to go around.

c.   improper power application.

d.   failure to control pitch attitude.

e.   failure to compensate for torque effect.

f.   improper trim technique.

g.   failure to maintain recommended airspeeds.

h.   improper wing flaps or landing gear retraction procedure.

i.   failure to maintain proper track during climb-out.

j.   failure to remain well clear of obstructions and other traffic.

3.   Demonstrates and simultaneously explains a go-around/ rejected landing from an instructional standpoint.

4.   Analyzes and corrects simulated common errors related to a go-around/rejected landing.

Task G: Short-Field (Confined Area (AMES)) Approach and Landing (AMEL and AMES)

References: *FAA-H-8083-3, FAA-H-8083-23, FAA-S-8081-12, FAA-S-ACS-6; POH/AFM.*

Objective: To determine that the applicant:

1.   Exhibits instructional knowledge of the elements of a short-field approach and landing by describing:

a.   how to determine landing performance and limitations.

b.   configuration and trim.

c.   proper use of pitch and power to maintain desired approach angle.

d.   barriers and other hazards which should be considered.

e.   effect of wind.

f.   selection of touchdown and go-around points.

g.   a stabilized approach at the recommended airspeed to the selected touchdown point.

h.   coordination of flight controls.

i.   a precise ground track.

j. timing, judgment, and control procedure during roundout and touchdown.
k. directional control after touchdown.
l. use of brakes (landplane).
m. use of checklist.
n. after landing runway incursion procedures.

2. Exhibits instructional knowledge of common errors related to a short-field approach and landing by describing:

a. improper use of landing performance data and limitations.
b. failure to establish approach and landing configuration at appropriate time or in proper sequence.
c. failure to establish and maintain a stabilized approach.
d. improper technique in use of power, wing flaps, and trim.
e. inappropriate removal of hand from throttles.
f. improper procedure during roundout and touchdown.
g. poor directional control after touchdown.
h. improper use of brakes (landplane).

3. Demonstrates and simultaneously explains a short-field approach and landing from an instructional standpoint.
4. Analyzes and corrects simulated common errors related to a short-field approach and landing.

Task H: Glassy-Water Approach and Landing (AMES)

References: FAA-H-8083-3, FAA-H-8083-23, FAA-S-8081-12, FAA-S-ACS-6; POH/AFM.

Objective: To determine that the applicant:

1. Exhibits instructional knowledge of the elements of a glassy-water approach and landing by describing:

a. how to determine landing performance and limitations.
b. configuration and trim.
c. deceptive characteristics of glassy water.
d. selection of a suitable landing area and go-around point.
e. terrain and obstructions which should be considered.
f. detection of hazards in the landing area such as shallow water, obstructions, or floating debris.
g. coordination of flight controls.
h. a precise ground track.
i. a power setting and pitch attitude that will result in the recommended airspeed and rate of descent throughout the final approach to touchdown.

j.   how to maintain positive after landing control.
k.   use of checklist.

2.   Exhibits instructional knowledge of common errors related to a glassy-water approach and landing by describing:

a.   improper use of landing performance data and limitations.
b.   failure to establish approach and landing configuration at appropriate time and in proper sequence.
c.   failure to establish and maintain a stabilized approach at the recommended airspeed and rate of descent.
d.   improper technique in use of power, wing flaps, or trim.
e.   inappropriate removal of hand from throttles.
f.   failure to touch down with power in the proper stabilized attitude.
g.   failure to maintain positive control after landing.

3.   Demonstrates and simultaneously explains a glassy-water approach and landing from an instructional standpoint.
4.   Analyzes and corrects simulated common errors related to a glassy-water approach and landing.

Task I: Rough-Water Approach and Landing (AMES)

References: FAA-H-8083-3, FAA-H-8083-23, FAA-S-8081-12, FAA-S-ACS-6; POH/AFM.

Objective: To determine that the applicant:

1.   Exhibits instructional knowledge of the elements of a rough-water approach and landing by describing:

a.   how to determine landing performance and limitations.
b.   review of wind conditions.
c.   how landing area characteristics can be evaluated.
d.   selection of a suitable landing area and go-around point.
e.   terrain and obstructions which should be considered.
f.   detection of hazards in the landing area such as shallow water, obstructions, or floating debris.
g.   configuration and trim.
h.   coordination of flight controls.
i.   a precise ground track.
j.   a stabilized approach at the recommended airspeed to the selected touchdown area.
k.   timing, judgment, and control procedure during roundout and touchdown.
l.   maintenance of positive after landing control.
m.   use of checklist.

2. Exhibits instructional knowledge of common errors related to a rough-water approach and landing by describing:

    a. improper use of landing performance data and limitations.
    b. failure to establish approach and landing configuration at appropriate time and in proper sequence.
    c. failure to establish and maintain a stabilized approach.
    d. improper procedure in use of power, wing flaps, or trim.
    e. inappropriate removal of hand from throttles.
    f. improper procedure during roundout and touchdown.
    g. failure to maintain positive control after landing.

3. Demonstrates and simultaneously explains a rough-water approach and landing from an instructional standpoint.
4. Analyzes and corrects simulated common errors related a rough-water approach and landing.

VIII. Fundamentals of Flight

Note: *The examiner must select at least one Task.*

Task A: Straight-and-Level Flight (AMEL and AMES)

References: FAA-H-8083-3, FAA-H-8083-2, FAA-S-ACS-6.

Objective: To determine that the applicant:

1. Exhibits instructional knowledge of the elements of straight-and-level flight by describing:

   a. effect and use of flight controls.
   b. the Integrated Flight Instruction method.
   c. outside and instrument references used for pitch, bank, yaw, and power control; the crosscheck and interpretation of those references; and the control technique used.
   d. trim technique.
   e. methods that can be used to overcome tenseness and over controlling.

2. Exhibits instructional knowledge of common errors related to straight-and-level flight by describing:

   a. failure to cross-check and correctly interpret outside and instrument references.
   b. application of control movements rather than pressures.
   c. uncoordinated use of flight controls.
   d. faulty trim technique.

3. Demonstrates and simultaneously explains straight-and-level flight from an instructional standpoint.
4. Analyzes and corrects simulated common errors related to straight-and-level flight.

Task B: Level Turns (AMEL and AMES)

References: FAA-H-8083-3, FAA-S-ACS-6.

Objective: To determine that the applicant:

1. Exhibits instructional knowledge of the elements of level turns by describing:

   a. effect and use of flight controls.
   b. the Integrated Flight Instruction method.

     c.   outside and instrument references used for pitch, bank, yaw, and power control; the crosscheck and interpretation of those references; and the control technique used.

     d.   trim technique.

     e.   methods that can be used to overcome tenseness and over controlling.

2.   Exhibits instructional knowledge of common errors related to level turns by describing:

     a.   failure to cross-check and correctly interpret outside and instrument references.

     b.   application of control movements rather than pressures.

     c.   uncoordinated use of flight controls.

     d.   faulty altitude and bank control.

3.   Demonstrates and simultaneously explains a level turn from an instructional standpoint.

4.   Analyzes and corrects simulated common errors related to level turns.

Task C: Straight Climbs and Climbing Turns (AMEL and AMES)

References: FAA-H-8083-3, FAA-S-ACS-6.

Objective: To determine that the applicant:

1.   Exhibits instructional knowledge of the elements of straight climbs and climbing turns by describing:

     a.   effect and use of flight controls.

     b.   the Integrated Flight Instruction method.

     c.   outside and instrument references used for pitch, bank, yaw, and power control; the cross-check and interpretation of those references; and the control technique used.

     d.   trim technique.

     e.   methods that can be used to overcome tenseness and over controlling.

2.   Exhibits instructional knowledge of common errors related to straight climbs and climbing turns by describing:

     a.   failure to cross-check and correctly interpret outside and instrument references.

     b.   application of control movements rather than pressures.

    c.   improper correction for torque effect.

    d.   faulty trim technique.

3.   Demonstrates and simultaneously explains straight climbs and a climbing turns from an instructional standpoint.

4.   Analyzes and corrects simulated common errors related to straight climbs and climbing turns.

Task D: Straight Descents and Descending Turns (AMEL and AMES)

References: FAA-H-8083-3, FAA-S-ACS-6.

Objective: To determine that the applicant:

1.   Exhibits instructional knowledge of the elements of straight descents and descending turns by describing:

    a.   effect and use of flight controls.

    b.   the Integrated Flight Instruction method.

    c.   outside and instrument references used for pitch, bank, yaw, and power control; the cross-check and interpretation of those references; and the control technique used.

    d.   trim technique.

    e.   methods that can be used to overcome tenseness and over controlling.

2.   Exhibits instructional knowledge of common errors related to straight descents and descending turns by describing:

    a.   failure to cross-check and correctly interpret outside and instrument references.

    b.   application of control movements rather than pressures.

    c.   uncoordinated use of flight controls.

    d.   faulty trim technique.

    e.   failure to clear engine and use carburetor heat, as appropriate.

3.   Demonstrates and simultaneously explains straight descents and descending turns from an instructional standpoint.

4.   Analyzes and corrects simulated common errors related to straight descents and descending turns.

IX.   Performance Maneuvers

Task A: Steep Turns (AMEL and AMES)

References: FAA-H-8083-3, FAA-S-8081-12, FAA-S-ACS-6;
POH/AFM.

Objective: To determine that the applicant:

1.   Exhibits instructional knowledge of the elements of steep turns by describing:

   a.   relationship of bank angle, load factor, and stalling speed.
   b.   overbanking tendency.
   c.   torque effect in right and left turns.
   d.   selection of a suitable altitude.
   e.   orientation, division of attention, and planning.
   f.   entry and rollout procedure.
   g.   coordination of flight and power controls.
   h.   altitude, bank, and power control during the turn.
   i.   proper recovery to straight-and-level flight.

2.   Exhibits instructional knowledge of common errors related to steep turns by describing:

   a.   improper pitch, bank, and power coordination during entry and rollout.
   b.   uncoordinated use of flight controls.
   c.   improper procedure in correcting altitude deviations.
   d.   loss of orientation.

3.   Demonstrates and simultaneously explains steep turns from an instructional standpoint.
4.   Analyzes and corrects simulated common errors related to steep turns.

X. Ground Reference Maneuvers

Note: *The examiner must select at least one Task.*

Task A: *Rectangular Course (AMEL and AMES)*

References: FAA-H-8083-3, FAA-S-ACS-6.

Objective: To determine that the applicant:

1. Exhibits instructional knowledge of the elements of a rectangular course by describing:

   a. how to select a safe altitude.
   b. how to select a suitable ground reference with consideration given to emergency landing areas.
   c. orientation, division of attention, and planning.
   d. configuration and airspeed prior to entry.
   e. relationship of a rectangular course to an airport traffic pattern.
   f. wind drift correction.
   g. how to maintain desired altitude, airspeed, and distance from ground reference boundaries.
   h. timing of turn entries and rollouts.
   i. coordination of flight controls.

2. Exhibits instructional knowledge of common errors related to a rectangular course by describing:

   a. poor planning, orientation, or division of attention.
   b. uncoordinated use of flight controls.
   c. improper correction for wind drift.
   d. failure to maintain selected altitude or airspeed.
   e. selection of a ground reference where there is no suitable emergency landing area within gliding distance.

3. Demonstrates and simultaneously explains a rectangular course from an instructional standpoint.
4. Analyzes and corrects simulated common errors related to a rectangular course.

Task B: *S-Turns Across a Road (AMEL and AMES)*

References: FAA-H-8083-3, FAA-S-ACS-6.

Objective: To determine that the applicant:

1. Exhibits instructional knowledge of the elements of S-turns across a road by describing:

a. how to select a safe altitude.
b. how to select a suitable ground reference line with consideration given to emergency landing areas.
c. orientation, division of attention, and planning.
d. configuration and airspeed prior to entry.
e. entry procedure.
f. wind drift correction.
g. tracking of semicircles of equal radii on either side of the selected ground reference line.
h. how to maintain desired altitude and airspeed.
i. turn reversal over the ground reference line.
j. coordination of flight controls.

2. Exhibits instructional knowledge of common errors related to S-turns across a road by describing:

a. faulty entry technique.
b. poor planning, orientation, or division of attention.
c. uncoordinated use of flight controls.
d. improper correction for wind drift.
e. an unsymmetrical ground track.
f. failure to maintain selected altitude or airspeed.
g. selection of a ground reference line where there is no suitable emergency landing area within gliding distance.

3. Demonstrates and simultaneously explains S-turns across a road from an instructional standpoint.
4. Analyzes and corrects simulated common errors related to S-turns across a road.

Task C: Turns Around a Point (AMEL and AMES)

References: FAA-H-8083-3, FAA-S-ACS-6.

Objective: To determine that the applicant:

1. Exhibits instructional knowledge of the elements of turns around a point by describing:

a. how to select a safe altitude.
b. how to select a suitable ground reference point with consideration given to emergency landing areas.
c. orientation, division of attention, and planning.
d. configuration and airspeed prior to entry.
e. entry procedure.
f. wind drift correction.
g. how to maintain desired altitude, airspeed, and distance from reference point.
h. coordination of flight controls.

2.	Exhibits instructional knowledge of common errors related to turns around a point by describing:

   a.	faulty entry procedure.
   b.	poor planning, orientation, or division of attention.
   c.	uncoordinated use of flight controls.
   d.	improper correction for wind drift.
   e.	failure to maintain selected altitude or airspeed.
   f.	selection of a ground reference point where there is no suitable emergency landing area within gliding distance.

3.	Demonstrates and simultaneously explains turns around a point from an instructional standpoint.
4.	Analyzes and corrects simulated common errors related to turns around a point.

XI.   Slow Flight and Stalls

Note: *The examiner must select at least one Task. Stalls must not be performed with one engine at reduced power or inoperative and the other engine(s) developing effective power.*

Stalls using high power settings should not be performed. The high pitch angles necessary to induce these stalls could possibly result in uncontrollable flight.

Examiners and instructors should be alert to the possible development of high sink rates when performing stalls in multiengine airplanes with high wing loading.

Task A: Maneuvering During Slow Flight (AMEL and AMES)

References: *FAA-H-8083-3, FAA-S-8081-12, FAA-S-ACS-6; POH/AFM.*

Objective: To determine that the applicant:

1.   Exhibits instructional knowledge of the elements of maneuvering during slow flight by describing:

   a.   relationship of configuration, weight, center of gravity, maneuvering loads, angle of bank, and power to flight characteristics and controllability.
   b.   relationship of the maneuver to critical flight situations, such as go-arounds.
   c.   performance of the maneuver with selected landing gear and flap configurations in straight-and-level flight and level turns.
   d.   specified airspeed for the maneuver.
   e.   coordination of flight controls.
   f.   trim technique.
   g.   reestablishment of cruise flight.

2.   Exhibits instructional knowledge of common errors related to maneuvering during slow flight by describing:

   a.   failure to establish specified gear and flap configuration.
   b.   improper entry technique.
   c.   failure to establish and maintain the specified airspeed.
   d.   excessive variations of altitude and heading when a constant altitude and heading are specified.
   e.   rough and/or uncoordinated use of flight controls.

f.	improper correction for torque effect.
g.	improper trim technique.
h.	unintentional stalls.
i.	inappropriate removal of hand from throttles.

3.	Demonstrates and simultaneously explains maneuvering during slow flight from an instructional standpoint.
4.	Analyzes and corrects simulated common errors related to maneuvering during slow flight.

## Task B:	Power-On Stalls (AMEL and AMES)

*References:	FAA-H-8083-3, FAA-S-8081-12, FAA-S-ACS-6; POH/AFM.*

Objective:	To determine that the applicant:

1.	Exhibits instructional knowledge of the elements of power-on stalls, in climbing flight (straight or turning), with selected landing gear and flap configurations by describing:

a.	aerodynamics of power-on stalls.
b.	relationship of various factors, such as landing gear and flap configuration, weight, center of gravity, load factor, and bank angle to stall speed.
c.	flight situations where unintentional power-on stalls may occur.
d.	entry technique and minimum entry altitude.
e.	performance of power-on stalls in climbing flight (straight or turning).
f.	coordination of flight controls.
g.	recognition of the first indications of power-on stalls.
h.	recovery technique and minimum recovery altitude.

2.	Exhibits instructional knowledge of common errors related to power-on stalls, in climbing flight (straight or turning), with selected landing gear and flap configurations by describing:

a.	failure to establish the specified landing gear and flap configuration prior to entry.
b.	improper pitch, bank, and yaw control during straight-ahead stalls.
c.	improper pitch, bank, and yaw control during turning stalls.
d.	rough and/or uncoordinated use of flight controls.
e.	failure to recognize the first indications of a stall.
f.	failure to achieve a stall.
g.	improper torque correction.
h.	poor stall recognition and delayed recovery.

i.   excessive altitude loss or excessive airspeed during recovery.

j.   secondary stall during recovery.

3.   Demonstrates and simultaneously explains power-on stalls, in climbing flight (straight or turning), with selected landing gear and flap configurations, from an instructional standpoint.

4.   Analyzes and corrects simulated common errors related to power-on stalls, in climbing flight (straight and turning), with selected landing gear and flap configurations.

Task C: *Power-Off Stalls (AMEL and AMES)*

References: FAA-H-8083-3, FAA-S-8081-12, FAA-S-ACS-6; POH/AFM.

Objective: To determine that the applicant:

1.   Exhibits instructional knowledge of the elements of power-off stalls, in descending flight (straight or turning), with selected landing gear and flap configurations by describing:

a.   aerodynamics of power-off stalls.

b.   relationship of various factors, such as landing gear and flap configuration, weight, center of gravity, load factor, and bank angle to stall speed.

c.   flight situations where unintentional power-off stalls may occur.

d.   entry technique and minimum entry altitude.

e.   performance of power-off stalls in descending flight (straight or turning).

f.   coordination of flight controls.

g.   recognition of the first indications of power-off stalls.

h.   recovery technique and minimum recovery altitude.

2.   Exhibits instructional knowledge of common errors related to power-off stalls, in descending flight (straight or turning), with selected landing gear and flap configurations by describing:

a.   failure to establish the specified landing gear and flap configuration prior to entry.

b.   improper pitch, yaw, and bank control during straight-ahead stalls.

c.   improper pitch, yaw, and bank control during turning stalls.

d.   rough and/or uncoordinated use of flight controls.

e.   failure to recognize the first indications of a stall.

f.   failure to achieve a stall.

g.   improper torque correction.
h.   poor stall recognition and delayed recovery.
i.   excessive altitude loss or excessive airspeed during recovery.
j.   secondary stall during recovery.

3.   Demonstrates and simultaneously explains power-off stalls, in descending flight (straight or turning), with selected landing gear and flap configurations, from an instructional standpoint.
4.   Analyzes and corrects simulated common errors related to power-off stalls, in descending flight (straight or turning), with selected landing gear and flap configurations.

Task D: Accelerated Maneuver Stalls (Demonstration) (AMEL and AMES)

Note: *This Task can either be completed by oral examination or demonstrated at examiner's discretion.*

References: FAA-H-8083-3; POH/AFM.

Objective: To determine that the applicant:

1.   Exhibits instructional knowledge of the elements of accelerated maneuver stalls by describing:

    a.   aerodynamics of accelerated maneuver stalls.
    b.   flight situations where accelerated maneuver stalls may occur.
    c.   hazards of accelerated stalls during stall or spin recovery.
    d.   entry procedure and minimum entry altitude.
    e.   recognition of the accelerated stall.
    f.   recovery procedure and minimum recovery altitude.

2.   Demonstrates and simultaneously explains accelerated maneuver stall, from an instructional standpoint:
3.   Exhibits instructional knowledge of common errors related to accelerated maneuver stalls by describing:

    a.   failure to establish proper configuration prior to entry.
    b.   improper or inadequate demonstration of the recognition of and recovery from an accelerated maneuver stall.
    c.   failure to present simulated student instruction that adequately emphasizes the hazards of poor procedures in recovering from an accelerated stall.

4. Analyzes and corrects simulated common errors related to accelerated stalls.

XII. Basic Instrument Maneuvers

Note: *The examiner must select at least one Task.*

Task A: *Straight-and-Level Flight (AMEL and AMES)*

References: FAA-H-8083-3, FAA-H-8083-15, FAA-S-ACS-6.

Objective: To determine that the applicant:

1. Exhibits instructional knowledge of the elements of straight-and-level flight, solely by reference to instruments by describing:

   a. instrument cross-check, instrument interpretation, and aircraft control.
   b. instruments used for pitch, bank, and power control, and how those instruments are used to maintain altitude, heading, and airspeed.
   c. trim technique.

2. Exhibits instructional knowledge of common errors related to straight-and-level flight solely by reference to instruments by describing:

   a. "fixation," "omission," and "emphasis" errors during instrument cross-check.
   b. improper instrument interpretation.
   c. improper control applications.
   d. failure to establish proper pitch, bank, or power adjustments during altitude, heading, or airspeed corrections.
   e. faulty trim technique.

3. Demonstrates and simultaneously explains straight-and-level flight, solely by reference to instruments, from an instructional standpoint.
4. Analyzes and corrects simulated common errors related to straight-and-level flight, solely by reference to instruments.

Task B: *Constant Airspeed Climbs (AMEL and AMES)*

References: FAA-H-8083-3, FAA-H-8083-15, FAA-S-ACS-6.

Objective: To determine that the applicant:

1. Exhibits instructional knowledge of the elements of straight and turning, constant airspeed climbs, solely by reference to instruments by describing:

    a.   instrument cross-check, instrument interpretation, and aircraft control.

    b.   instruments used for pitch, bank, and power control during entry, during the climb, and during level off, and how those instruments are used to maintain climb heading and airspeed.

    c.   trim technique.

2.   Exhibits instructional knowledge of common errors related to straight and turning, constant airspeed climbs, solely by reference to instruments by describing:

    a.   "fixation," "omission," and "emphasis" errors during instrument cross-check.

    b.   improper instrument interpretation.

    c.   improper control applications.

    d.   failure to establish proper pitch, bank, or power adjustments during heading and airspeed corrections.

    e.   improper entry or level-off technique.

    f.   faulty trim technique.

3.   Demonstrates and simultaneously explains a straight, constant airspeed climb, solely by reference to instruments, from an instructional standpoint.

4.   Analyzes and corrects simulated common errors related to straight, constant airspeed climbs, solely by reference to instruments.

Task C: Constant Airspeed Descents (AMEL and AMES)

References: *FAA-H-8083-3, FAA-H-8083-15, FAA-S-ACS-6.*

Objective: To determine that the applicant:

1.   Exhibits instructional knowledge of the elements of straight and turning, constant airspeed descents, solely by reference to instruments by describing:

    a.   instrument cross-check, instrument interpretation, and aircraft control.

    b.   instruments used for pitch, bank, and power control during entry, during the descent, and during level off, and how those instruments are used to maintain descent heading and airspeed.

    c.   trim technique.

2.   Exhibits instructional knowledge of common errors related to straight and turning, constant airspeed descents, solely by reference to instruments by describing:

a. "fixation," "omission," and "emphasis" errors during instrument cross-check.
b. improper instrument interpretation.
c. improper control applications.
d. failure to establish proper pitch, bank, or power adjustments during heading and airspeed corrections.
e. improper entry or level-off technique.
f. faulty trim technique.

3. Demonstrates and simultaneously explains a straight, constant airspeed descent, solely by reference to instruments, from an instructional standpoint.
4. Analyzes and corrects simulated common errors related to straight, constant airspeed descents, solely by reference to instruments.

Task D: Turns to Headings (AMEL and AMES)

References: FAA-H-8083-3, FAA-H-8083-15, FAA-S-ACS-6.

Objective: To determine that the applicant:

1. Exhibits instructional knowledge of the elements of turns to headings, solely by reference to instruments by describing:

   a. instrument cross-check, instrument interpretation, and aircraft control.
   b. instruments used for pitch, bank, and power control during turn entry, during the turn, and during the turn rollout, and how those instruments are used.
   c. trim technique.

2. Exhibits instructional knowledge of common errors related to turns to headings, solely by reference to instruments by describing:

   a. "fixation," "omission," and "emphasis" errors during instrument cross-check.
   b. improper instrument interpretation.
   c. improper control applications.
   d. failure to establish proper pitch, bank, and power adjustments during altitude, bank, and airspeed corrections.
   e. improper entry or rollout technique.
   f. faulty trim technique.

3. Demonstrates and simultaneously explains a turn to a heading, solely by reference to instruments, from an instructional standpoint.

4. Analyzes and corrects simulated common errors related to turns to headings, solely by reference to instruments.

Task E: *Recovery from Unusual Flight Attitudes (AMEL and AMES)*

References: FAA-H-8083-3, FAA-H-8083-15, FAA-S-ACS-6.

Objective: To determine that the applicant:

1. Exhibits instructional knowledge of the elements of recovery from unusual flight attitudes by describing:

   a. conditions and situations that may result in unusual flight attitudes.
   b. the two basic unusual flight attitudes—nose-high (climbing turn) and nose-low (diving spiral).
   c. how unusual flight attitudes are recognized.
   d. control sequence for recovery from a nose-high attitude and the reasons for that sequence.
   e. control sequence for recovery from a nose-low attitude and the reasons for that sequence.
   f. reasons why the controls should be coordinated during unusual flight attitude recoveries.

2. Exhibits instructional knowledge of common errors related to recovery from unusual flight attitudes by describing:

   a. failure to recognize an unusual flight attitude.
   b. consequences of attempting to recover from an unusual flight attitude by "feel" rather than by instrument indications.
   c. inappropriate control applications during recovery.
   d. failure to recognize from instrument indications when the airplane is passing through a level flight attitude.

3. Demonstrates and simultaneously explains recovery from a nose-high and a nose-low unusual flight attitude from an instructional standpoint.
4. Analyzes and corrects simulated common errors related to recovery from unusual flight attitudes.

XIII. Emergency Operations

Note: The examiner shall select Tasks B or C, D, and one other Task.

Task A: Systems and Equipment Malfunctions (AMEL and AMES)

References: FAA-H-8083-3; FAA-S-8081-12, FAA-S-ACS-6; POH/AFM.

Note: The examiner must not simulate a system or equipment malfunction in a manner that may jeopardize safe flight or result in possible damage to the airplane.

Objective: To determine that the applicant exhibits instructional knowledge of the elements related to systems and equipment malfunctions, appropriate to the airplane used for the practical test, by describing recommended pilot action for at least five (5) of the following:

1. Smoke, fire, or both, during ground or flight operations
2. Rough running engine, partial power loss, or sudden engine stoppage
3. Propeller malfunction
4. Loss of engine oil pressure
5. Fuel starvation
6. Engine overheat
7. Hydraulic system malfunction
8. Electrical system malfunction
9. Carburetor or induction icing
10. Door or window opening in flight
11. Inoperative or "runaway" trim
12. Landing gear or flap malfunction
13. Pressurization malfunction

Task B: Engine Failure During Takeoff Before V$_{MC}$ (AMEL and AMES)

Note: Engine failure must not be simulated at a speed greater than 50 percent V$_{MC}$.

References: FAA-H-8083-3, FAA-S-8081-12, FAA-S-ACS-6; POH/AFM.

Objective: To determine that the applicant:

1. Exhibits instructional knowledge of the elements related to engine failure during takeoff before V_{MC} by describing:

   a. use of prescribed emergency procedure.
   b. prompt closing of throttles.
   c. how to maintain directional control.
   d. proper use of brakes (landplane).

2. Exhibits instructional knowledge of common errors related to engine failure during takeoff before V_{MC} by describing:

   a. failure to follow prescribed emergency procedure.
   b. failure to promptly recognize engine failure.
   c. failure to promptly close throttles following engine failure.
   d. faulty directional control and use of brakes.

3. Demonstrates and simultaneously explains a simulated engine failure during takeoff before V_{MC} from an instructional standpoint.
4. Analyzes and corrects simulated common errors related to engine failure during takeoff before V_{MC}.

Task C: Engine Failure After Lift-Off (AMEL and AMES)

References: FAA-H-8083-3, FAA-S-8081-12, FAA-S-ACS-6; POH/AFM.

Objective: To determine that the applicant:

1. Exhibits instructional knowledge of the elements related to engine failure after lift-off by describing:

   a. use of prescribed emergency checklist to verify accomplishment of procedures for securing the inoperative engine.
   b. proper adjustment of engine controls, reduction of drag, and identification and verification of the inoperative engine.
   c. how to establish and maintain a pitch attitude that will result in the best engine inoperative airspeed, considering the height of obstructions.
   d. how to establish and maintain a bank as required for best performance.
   e. how to maintain directional control.
   f. methods to be used for determining reason for malfunction.
   g. monitoring and proper use of the operating engine.
   h. an emergency approach and landing, if a climb or level flight is not within the airplane's performance capability.

i.   positive airplane control.

j.   how to obtain assistance from the appropriate facility.

2.   Exhibits instructional knowledge of common errors related to engine failure after lift-off by describing:

    a.   failure to follow prescribed emergency checklist.
    b.   failure to properly identify and verify the inoperative engine.
    c.   failure to properly adjust engine controls and reduce drag.
    d.   failure to maintain directional control.
    e.   failure to establish and maintain a pitch attitude that will result in best engine inoperative airspeed, considering the height of obstructions.
    f.   failure to establish and maintain proper bank for best performance.

3.   Demonstrates and simultaneously explains a simulated engine failure after lift-off from an instructional standpoint.

4.   Analyzes and corrects simulated common errors related to engine failure after lift-off.

Task D: Approach and Landing with an Inoperative Engine (AMEL and AMES)

References: *FAA-H-8083-3, FAA-S-8081-12, FAA-S-ACS-6; POH/AFM.*

Objective: To determine that the applicant:

1.   Exhibits instructional knowledge of the elements related to an approach and landing with an inoperative engine by describing:

    a.   use of the prescribed emergency checklist to verify accomplishment of procedures for securing the inoperative engine.
    b.   proper adjustment of engine controls, reduction of drag, and identification and verification of the inoperative engine.
    c.   how to establish and maintain best engine inoperative airspeed.
    d.   trim procedure.
    e.   how to establish and maintain a bank as required for best performance.
    f.   the monitoring and adjusting of the operating engine.
    g.   proper approach to selected touchdown area, at the recommended airspeed.

h. proper application of flight controls.
i. how to maintain a precise ground track.
j. wind shear and turbulence.
k. proper timing, judgment, and control procedure during roundout and touchdown.
l. directional control after touchdown.
m. use of brakes (landplane).

2. Exhibits instructional knowledge of common errors related to an approach and landing with an inoperative engine by describing:

a. failure to follow prescribed emergency checklist.
b. failure to properly identify and verify the inoperative engine.
c. failure to properly adjust engine controls and reduce drag.
d. failure to establish and maintain best engine inoperative airspeed.
e. improper trim procedure.
f. failure to establish proper approach and landing configuration at appropriate time and in proper sequence.
g. failure to use proper procedure for wind shear or turbulence.
h. faulty technique during roundout and touchdown.
i. improper directional control after touchdown.
j. improper use of brakes (landplane).

3. Demonstrates and simultaneously explains an approach and landing with a simulated inoperative engine from an instructional standpoint.
4. Analyzes and corrects simulated common errors related to an approach and landing with an inoperative engine.

Task E: *Emergency Descent (AMEL and AMES)*

References: *FAA-H-8083-3, FAA-S-8081-12, FAA-S-ACS-6; POH/AFM.*

Objective: To determine that the applicant:

1. Exhibits instructional knowledge of the elements related to an emergency descent by describing:

a. situations that require an emergency descent.
b. proper use of the prescribed emergency checklist to verify accomplishment of procedures for initiating the emergency descent.

c. proper use of clearing procedures before initiating and during the emergency descent.
d. procedures for recovering from an emergency descent.
e. manufacturer's procedures.

2. Exhibits instructional knowledge of common errors related to an emergency descent by describing:

a. the consequences of failing to identify reason for executing an emergency descent.
b. improper use of the prescribed emergency checklist to verify accomplishment of procedures for initiating the emergency descent.
c. improper use of clearing procedures before initiating and during the emergency descent.
d. improper procedures for recovering from an emergency descent.

3. Demonstrates and simultaneously explains an approach and landing with a simulated inoperative engine from an instructional standpoint.
4. Analyzes and corrects simulated common errors related to an approach and landing with an inoperative engine.

Task F: Emergency Equipment and Survival Gear (AMEL and AMES)

References: FAA-H-8083-3, FAA-H-8083-23, FAA-S-8081-12, FAA-S-ACS-6; POH/AFM.

Objective: To determine that the applicant exhibits instructional knowledge of the elements related to emergency equipment and survival gear appropriate to the airplane flown by describing:

1. Equipment and gear appropriate for operation in various climates, over various types of terrain, and over water.
2. Purpose, method of operation or use, servicing and storage of appropriate equipment.

XIV. Multiengine Operations

Note: *The examiner must select Tasks D, E, and one other Task.*

Task A: *Operation of Systems (AMEL and AMES)*

References: *FAA-H-8083-3, FAA-S-8081-12, FAA-S-ACS-6;*
POH/AFM.

Objective: To determine that the applicant exhibits instructional
knowledge of the elements related to the operation of
systems, as applicable to the multiengine airplane
used for the practical test, by describing at least five
(5) of the following systems:

1.   Primary flight controls and trim
2.   Flaps, leading edge devices, and spoilers
3.   Water rudders
4.   Powerplant and propellers
5.   Landing gear
6.   Fuel, oil, and hydraulic system
7.   Electrical
8.   Avionics
9.   Pitot static/vacuum system and associated instruments
10.   Environmental.
11.   Deicing and anti-icing

Task B: *Performance and Limitations (AMEL and AMES)*

References: *FAA-H-8083-3, FAA-S-8081-12, FAA-S-ACS-6;*
POH/AFM.

Objective: To determine that the applicant exhibits instructional
knowledge of the elements related to multiengine
performance and limitations by describing:

1.   Determination of weight and balance condition.
2.   Use of performance charts, tables, and other data in
determining performance in various phases of flight.
3.   Effects of exceeding limitations.
4.   Effects of atmospheric conditions on performance.
5.   Factors to be considered in determining that the required
performance is within the airplane's single and multiengine
capabilities.

Task C: *Flight Principles—Engine Inoperative (AMEL and AMES)*

References: *FAA-H-8083-3, FAA-S-8081-12, FAA-S-ACS-6; POH/AFM.*

Objective: To determine that the applicant exhibits instructional knowledge of the elements related to flight principles engine—inoperative by describing:

1. Meaning of the term "critical engine."
2. Effects of density altitude on the V_{MC} demonstration.
3. Effects of airplane weight and center of gravity on control.
4. Effects of bank angle on V_{MC}.
5. Relationship of V_{MC} to stall speed.
6. Reasons for loss of directional control.
7. Indications of loss of directional control.
8. Importance of maintaining the proper pitch and bank attitude, and the proper coordination of controls.
9. Loss of directional control recovery procedures.
10. Engine failure during takeoff including planning, decisions, and single-engine operations.

Task D: Maneuvering with One Engine Inoperative (AMEL and AMES)

References: *FAA-H-8083-3, FAA-S-8081-12, FAA-S-ACS-6; POH/AFM.*

Note: *The feathering of one propeller can be demonstrated in any multiengine airplane equipped with propellers that can be safely feathered unless the manufacturer prohibits the intentional feathering of the propellers during flight. Feathering for pilot flight test purposes should be performed only under such conditions and at such altitudes (no lower than 3,000 feet above the surface) and positions where safe landings on established airports can be readily accomplished, in the event difficulty is encountered during unfeathering.*

At altitudes lower than 3,000 feet above the surface, simulated engine failure will be performed by throttling the engine and then establishing zero thrust.

In the event a propeller cannot be unfeathered during the practical test, it should be treated as an emergency.

Objective: To determine that the applicant:

1. Exhibits instructional knowledge of the elements related to maneuvering with one engine inoperative by describing:

a. flight characteristics and controllability associated with maneuvering with one engine inoperative.
b. use of prescribed emergency checklist to verify accomplishment of procedures for securing inoperative engine.
c. proper adjustment of engine controls, reduction of drag, and identification and verification of the inoperative engine.
d. how to establish and maintain the best engine inoperative airspeed.
e. proper trim procedure.
f. how to establish and maintain a bank, as required, for best performance.
g. appropriate methods to be used for determining the reason for the malfunction.
h. importance of establishing a heading toward the nearest suitable airport or seaplane base.
i. importance of monitoring and adjusting the operating engine.
j. performance of straight-and-level flight, turns, descents, and climbs, if the airplane is capable of those maneuvers under existing conditions.

2. Exhibits instructional knowledge of common errors related to maneuvering with one engine inoperative by describing:

a. failure to follow prescribed emergency checklist.
b. failure to recognize an inoperative engine.
c. hazards of improperly identifying and verifying the inoperative engine.
d. failure to properly adjust engine controls and reduce drag.
e. failure to establish and maintain the best engine inoperative airspeed.
f. improper trim procedure.
g. failure to establish and maintain proper bank for best performance.
h. failure to maintain positive control while maneuvering.
i. hazards of attempting flight contrary to the airplane's operating limitations.

3. Demonstrates and simultaneously explains maneuvering with one engine inoperative from an instructional standpoint.
4. Analyzes and corrects simulated common errors related to maneuvering with one engine inoperative.

Task E: V_{MC} Demonstration (AMEL and AMES)

References: FAA-H-8083-3, FAA-S-8081-12, FAA-S-ACS-6; POH/AFM.

Note: *Performing this maneuver by increasing pitch attitude to a high angle with both engines operating and then reducing power on the critical engine should be avoided. This technique is hazardous and may result in loss of aircraft control.*

Objective: To determine that the applicant:

1. Exhibits instructional knowledge of the elements related to V_{MC} demonstration by describing:

   a. causes of loss of directional control at airspeeds less than V_{MC}, the factors affecting V_{MC}, and the safe recovery procedures.
   b. establishment of airplane configuration, adjustment of power controls, and trim prior to the demonstration.
   c. establishment of engine inoperative pitch attitude and airspeed.
   d. establishment of a bank attitude as required for best performance.
   e. entry procedure to demonstrate loss of directional control.
   f. indications that enable a pilot to recognize loss of directional control.
   g. proper recovery procedure.

2. Exhibits instructional knowledge of common errors related to V_{MC} demonstration by describing:

   a. inadequate knowledge of the causes of loss of directional control at airspeeds less than V_{MC}, factors affecting V_{MC}, and safe recovery procedures.
   b. improper entry procedures, including pitch attitude, bank attitude, and airspeed.
   c. failure to recognize imminent loss of directional control.
   d. failure to use proper recovery procedure.

3. Demonstrates and simultaneously explains engine inoperative loss of directional control from an instructional standpoint.
4. Analyzes and corrects simulated common errors related to engine inoperative loss of directional control.

Task F: ***Demonstrating the Effects of Various Airspeeds and Configurations during Engine Inoperative Performance (AMEL and AMES)***

References: *FAA-H-8083-3, FAA-S-8081-12, FAA-S-ACS-6;*
POH/AFM.

Objective: To determine that the applicant:

1. Exhibits instructional knowledge of the elements related to the effects of various airspeeds and configurations during engine inoperative performance by describing:

   a. selection of proper altitude for the demonstration.
   b. proper entry procedure to include pitch attitude, bank attitude, and airspeed.
   c. effects on performance of airspeed changes at, above, and below V_{YSE}.
   d. effects on performance of various configurations:

      i. extension of landing gear.
      ii. extension of wing flaps.
      iii. extension of both landing gear and wing flaps.
      iv. wind milling of propeller on inoperative engine.

   e. airspeed control throughout the demonstration.
   f. proper control technique and procedures throughout the demonstration.

2. Exhibits instructional knowledge of common errors related to the effects of various airspeeds and configurations during engine inoperative performance by describing:

   a. inadequate knowledge of the effects of airspeeds above or below V_{YSE} and of various configurations on performance.
   b. improper entry procedures, including pitch attitude, bank attitude, and airspeed.
   c. improper airspeed control throughout the demonstration.
   d. rough and/or uncoordinated use of flight controls.
   e. improper procedures during resumption of cruise flight.

3. Demonstrates and simultaneously explains the effects of various airspeeds and configurations during engine inoperative performance from an instructional standpoint.

4. Analyzes and corrects simulated common errors related to the effects of various airspeeds and configurations during engine inoperative performance.

XV.   Postflight Procedures

Note: *The examiner shall select Task A and for ASES applicants at least one other Task.*

Task A: *Postflight Procedures (AMEL and AMES)*

References: FAA-H-8083-3, FAA-H-8083-23, FAA-S-8081-12, FAA-S-ACS-6; POH/AFM.

Objective: To determine that the applicant:

1.   Exhibits instructional knowledge of the elements of postflight procedures by describing:

   a.   parking procedure (landplane).
   b.   engine shutdown and securing cockpit.
   c.   deplaning passengers.
   d.   securing airplane.
   e.   postflight inspection.
   f.   refueling.

2.   Exhibits instructional knowledge of common errors related to postflight procedures by describing:

   a.   hazards resulting from failure to follow recommended procedures.
   b.   poor planning, improper procedure, or faulty judgment in performance of postflight procedures.

3.   Demonstrates and simultaneously explains postflight procedures from an instructional standpoint.
4.   Analyzes and corrects simulated common errors related to postflight procedures.

Task B: *Anchoring (AMES)*

References: FAA-H-8083-3, FAA-H-8083-23, FAA-S-8081-12, FAA-S-ACS-6; POH/AFM.

Objective: To determine that the applicant:

1.   Exhibits instructional knowledge of the elements of anchoring by describing:

   a.   how to select a suitable area for anchoring.
   b.   recommended procedure for anchoring in a lake, river, or tidal area.
   c.   number of anchors and lines to be used to ensure seaplane security in various conditions.

d. hazards to be avoided during anchors.
e. requirements for anchoring lights.

2. Exhibits instructional knowledge of common errors related to anchoring by describing:

   a. hazards resulting from failure to follow recommended anchoring procedures.
   b. consequences of poor planning, improper procedure, or poor judgment when anchoring.
   c. consequences of failure to use anchor lines of adequate length and strength to ensure seaplane security.

3. Demonstrates and simultaneously explains anchoring from an instructional standpoint.
4. Analyzes and corrects simulated common errors related to anchoring.

Task C: Docking and Mooring (AMES)

References: FAA-H-8083-3, FAA-H-8083-23, FAA-S-8081-12, FAA-S-ACS-6; POH/AFM.

Objective: To determine that the applicant:

1. Exhibits instructional knowledge of the elements of anchoring and mooring by describing:

   a. how to select a suitable area for docking and mooring.
   b. recommended procedure for mooring in a lake, river, or tidal area.
   c. number of tie-downs and lines to be used to ensure seaplane security in various conditions.
   d. hazards to be avoided during docking and mooring.
   e. requirements for docking and mooring lights.

2. Exhibits instructional knowledge of common errors related to docking and mooring by describing:

   a. hazards resulting from failure to follow recommended procedures.
   b. consequences of poor planning, improper procedure, or poor judgment when docking and mooring.
   c. consequences of failure to use docking or mooring lines of adequate length and strength to ensure seaplane security.

3. Demonstrates and simultaneously explains docking and mooring from an instructional standpoint.

4. Analyzes and corrects simulated common errors related to docking and mooring.

Task D: Beaching (AMES)

References: *FAA-H-8083-3, FAA-H-8083-23, FAA-S-8081-12, FAA-S-ACS-6; POH/AFM.*

Objective: To determine that the applicant:

1. Exhibits instructional knowledge of the elements of beaching by describing:

    a. recommended procedures for beaching.
    b. factors to be considered such as beach selection, water depth, current, tide, and wind.
    c. procedures to be followed to ensure seaplane security.
    d. hazards to be avoided.

2. Exhibits instructional knowledge of common errors related to beaching by describing:

    a. hazards resulting from failure to follow recommended procedures.
    b. consequences of poor beach selection, poor planning, improper procedure, or faulty judgment when beaching.
    c. a consequence of failure to take appropriate precautions to avoid hazards or to ensure that seaplane is secure.

3. Demonstrates and simultaneously explains beaching from an instructional standpoint.
4. Analyzes and corrects simulated common errors related to beaching.

Task E: Ramping (AMES)

References: *FAA-H-8083-3, FAA-H-8083-23, FAA-S-8081-12, FAA-S-ACS-6; POH/AFM.*

Objective: To determine that the applicant:

1. Exhibits instructional knowledge of the elements of ramping by describing:

    a. factors, such as type of ramp surface, wind, current, and direction and control of approach speed.
    b. recommended procedures for ramping.
    c. hazards to be avoided.

2. Exhibits instructional knowledge of common errors related to ramping by describing:

    a. hazards resulting from failure to follow recommended procedures.
    b. consequences of poor planning, improper procedure, or faulty judgment when ramping.
    c. consequences of failure to take appropriate precautions to avoid hazards or to ensure that the seaplane is secure.

3. Demonstrates and simultaneously explains ramping from an instructional standpoint.
4. Analyzes and corrects simulated common errors related to ramping.

Made in the USA
Monee, IL
17 December 2020

53969527R00105